THE SINGLE GIRL'S GUIDE TO
BUCHAREST

First edition 2017

CONTENTS

INTRODUCTION

The Single Girl's Guide to Bucharest is the guide I needed myself when travelling solo to new countries. There are some great guidebooks out there, but lets face it, a woman travelling alone is a strange beast - an object of curiosity, maybe pity, sometimes even lust. Negotiating the pleasures and pitfalls of being a lone woman abroad is very different from the experience of travelling as part of a group or couple.

I have lived in Bucharest for several years, so the Romanian capital was an obvious choice for this debut guide. I aimed to include everything you would find in a regular travel guide - an overview of the city and its history, walks through the most interesting areas, listings for accommodation, restaurants and cafes, and so on.

But I also tried to address some of the questions specific to single female travellers. Can you dine out alone or do you have to stay in and order room service? How do you get to know people if you don't have the option of hanging out in a bar? What clothes should you pack?

To help answer some of these questions I interviewed three Bucharest insiders - tour guide Ana-Maria Adamoae, fashion blogger Olivia Ioana Dejeu and matchmaker Oana Torora - for their tips on life and love in the city known affectionately as Little Paris.

This book is the pilot issue of the first Single Girl's Guide - I hope the first of many. In 2018, I will release an updated and expanded electronic version of the Single Girl's Guide to Bucharest. If you like what you read, send an email to sgg2bucharest@gmail.com and I will let you know when the updated version can be downloaded for free.

Bon voyage!

Emily Blanchland

ABOUT BUCHAREST

Arriving in Bucharest from Henri Coanda Airport is to see the city at its best. The wide boulevard from the airport (the metro doesn't extend this far north yet) cuts a swathe through the verdant parks on the outskirts of the city. Cars and buses swoop around the Triumphal Arch, modelled on Paris' Arc de Triomphe and highlighting Bucharest's status as "Little Paris or "Paris of the East", then through yet more parks to Piata Victoriei, where the government headquarters sits opposite the historic buildings hosting the peasant museum and natural history museum. From there, Calea Victoriei - Bucharest's most fashionable street for centuries - leads south towards the old town with its cobbled streets and vibrant nightlife.

The old town, or Lipscani district, is perhaps the most visible evidence of the changes that have taken place over the last couple of decades. Romania remains one of the poorest countries in the EU, richer only than neighbouring Bulgaria. But the changes since Romania entered the bloc a decade ago have been dramatic. The once seedy and decrepit old town has had a facelift, and trendy bars and restaurants now spill out onto the narrow streets for most of the year.

This cafe culture is one of Bucharest's biggest attractions. Bucharest is also a cultural city, with myriad tiny art galleries hidden among the cafes and shops in the centre, in addition to the more significant art museums. Bookshops are ubiquitous; there are many street booksellers especially around the university area and even vending machines for books in the metro.

This all adds up to a city whose somewhat negative international image is undeserved. While visitor numbers are increasing, Bucharest is nowhere near being a tourist hub like other East European cities such as Prague or Budapest. Admittedly the hotchpotch of architectural styles, with many buildings blackened by pollution or close to collapse, lacks the appeal of other regional capitals or cities in nearby Transylvania. Communist dictator Nicolae Ceausescu's wholesale destruction of historic districts and their replacement with densely packed concrete apartment blocks left its indelible mark on large areas of the city.

But Bucharest's raffish appearance belies a city that is actually among the safest capitals in Europe. It's easy to get around too, with an extensive bus, tram and trolleybus network covering the areas not served by the four metro lines. Prices are relatively low, so paying for a single room isn't as painful as in more popular tourist hotspots.

Not only that, Bucharest's relative lack of obvious attractions means a visit to the city is a voyage of discovery. Stumble upon tiny churches and the ruins of the ancient princely court among the bars and strip joints of the old town. Sip coffee or a beer at backstreet bars with quirky decor and live jazz, or in the summer gardens in abandoned lots where tourists, artists and young families while away sunny afternoons together. Take a boat trip on Herestrau lake amid the lush greenery of the surrounding park.

Of course, there are some must see sights like the Palace of the Parliament (the world's second largest building) and the former Royal Palace that now houses the main art gallery, but overall, Bucharest is more a state of mind than a tourist destination.

It also stands out among fellow East European capitals for its funky urban vibe. In fact, after a couple of centuries being known as "Little Paris", the music festivals, underground clubs and growing hipster scene are rapidly earning it the monicker of the "New Berlin".

HISTORY

Archaeological research has shown that the Bucharest area
has been inhabited since the Paleolithic era. Numerous
Neolithic settlements have been uncovered in the area,
including one of the largest cemeteries in Europe.
Inhabited by the local Dacians, Thracian tribes, present
day Romania was conquered first by the ancient Greeks,
and later by the Romans in the early second century AD.

The name Bucharest supposedly comes from Bucur, a
quasi-mythical shepherd said to have founded the city.

In fact, the first definite record of Bucharest dates back to
the charter of 1459, a document that was discovered
around 1900. The charter was signed by Vlad Tepes, better
known as Vlad the Impaler or Dracula, who ruled the
Wallachia region - the southern part of present day
Romania where Bucharest is located.

Wallachia was absorbed into the Ottoman empire in 1417.
By 1600, all three regions of Romania - Moldavia,
Transylvania and Wallachia - were briefly united within
the Ottoman empire, but Transylvania was taken over by
the Hapsburg empire in 1687, while Wallachia (including
Bucharest) remained under Ottoman rule for the next four
centuries, with the exception of two brief periods of
Russian control.

Bucharest continued to expand through this time,
spreading westwards from the historic centre. As it grew, it
gradually eclipsed older centres of power such as nearby
Targoviste.

Despite its growing prominence, the 17th century was a
dark period for Bucharest. The city was devastated by the
1655 Seimenilor uprising and the great fire three years
later. In 1659, it was sacked by Tatars, before a two-year
drought caused famine across Romania.

However, the middle of the century also saw Bucharest again became the capital (in 1659), which marked the start of a period of rehabilitation and development, with large inns and churches being built in the city, and craftsmen's guilds established. The first Romanian school was opened in 1679.

Wallachia was united with Moldavia under Alexandru Ioan Cuza in 1859, and in 1862 the new state was named Romania. After Cuza was forced to abdicate, the German king Carol 1 took the throne.

Romania declared its independence from the Ottoman empire in 1877, triggering the brief war of independence.

The late 19th century was another period of intense development with the establishment of hospitals, museums and libraries. Western influence over clothing, language and institutions grew. France in particular was taken as a model for development, and this is when Bucharest was dubbed "Little Paris". In May 1857 Bucharest became the first city in the world to use oil lamps for street lighting. The University of Bucharest, the School of Beaux Arts and the first railway line between Bucharest and Giurgiu were all built during this period.

Romania's decision to enter the First World War on the Entente side in 1916 resulted in the post-war creation of Greater Romania, when Transylvania was finally brought under the control of Bucharest. Romania also included most of present-day Moldova.

Bucharest continued to expand in the inter-war period, with massive migration from rural areas to the capital, and cultural life flourished.

However, as the Second World War loomed, Romania, which had initially struck and alliance with France, found itself increasingly isolated in Eastern Europe, and was forced to give up territory. The government was overthrown and a fascist dictatorship loyal to Nazi

Germany was installed. Bucharest was bombed by Allied forces during the war, before switching sides in August 1944.

The same year, Romania like most of Eastern Europe became a communist satellite of the Soviet Union. Just two men ruled the country for the next four and a half decades; Gheorghe Gheorghiu from 1952 to 1965, then Nicolae Ceausescu until 1989.

Ceausescu initially made overtures to the west and managed to avoid involvement in the 1968 invasion of Czechoslovakia, despite pressure from Moscow. However, in the latter part of his rule he became increasingly erratic and megalomaniac - a switch that apparently dated from his visit to the North Korean capital Pyongyang in 1971. Romania was plunged into poverty and near starvation as Ceausescu diverted the country's resources abroad to pay off its debts. His rule also changed the face of Bucharest with many neighbourhoods demolished to make way for concrete apartment blocks and the giant Palace of the Parliament.

In 1989 communist regimes started to collapse across Eastern Europe. Romania was one of the last to fall, but mass demonstrations started in the Transylvanian city of Timisoara in December and quickly spread to Bucharest and other cities. After angry crowds surrounded the central committee building, Ceausescu and his wife Elena fled by helicopter but were captured and put on trial. They were executed on Christmas Day 1989.

The early years of independence were a struggle for Romanians, as they experienced the tough transition to a market economy. However, by the early 2000s, Romania was approaching EU membership (it entered the bloc in 2007), and the country's economy started to boom. Despite the setback of the 2008-2009 global crisis, and numerous political and corruption related crises domestically, 27 years after the fall of communism Bucharest has emerged as a modern European capital.

PROFILE: MARIE OF ROMANIA

Arguably Romania's best loved royal, Marie of Romania was born Princess Marie of Edinburgh in 1975 in Eastwell Park, Kent, to Prince Alfred, Duke of Edinburgh and Grand Duchess Maria Alexandrovna of Russia.

The blue-eyed, blonde-haired young princess attracted the attention of several royal bachelors including the Prince of Wales, and she was chosen as the wife of Crown Prince Ferdinand of Romania.

She was quickly taken to the hearts of the Romanian people, even though she had difficulty adjusting to life in her new homeland, her high spirits often clashing with the austere royal household. She was romantically linked to several men including Lieutenant Gheorghe Cantacuzène, Grand Duke Boris Vladimirovich of Russia, politician Waldorf Astor and Klondike miner Joe Boyle.

Romania entered the First World War on the Triple Entente, largely due to Marie's influence. During the war, she and her daughters worked acted as nurses in military hospitals in Moldavia.

In 1918, Marie vehemently opposed the signing of the Treaty of Bucharest with the Central Powers, which resulted in large land losses for Romania, giving rise to her description as "the only man in Romania". At the 1918 Paris Peace Conference at the end of the war, she lobbied for international recognition for Greater Romania.

After Ferdinand's death in 1926, a regency council was put in place until Ferdinand and Marie's grandson, King Michael, came of age. Her eldest son Carol had waived his rights to succession, but later deposed his son and took the throne. Threatened by Marie's popularity, he also removed his mother from political life. She spend the rest of her life alternating between the countryside and her home on the Black Sea coast, before dying of cirrhosis in 1938.

PROFILE: EUGENIA REUSS-IANCULESCU

Eugenia Reuss-Ianculescu was a leading suffragette and the co-founder of Romania's first women's suffrage organisation.

She was born into the aristocratic de Reuss-Mirza family in 1866, in the village of Igeşti, which at that time was part of the Austrian Empire. She grew up to become a teacher, travelling to France and Italy before marrying an army officer,

In 1889, Reuss-Ianculescu made her first attempt to set up a women's suffrage association, but failed due to lack of interest. After another failed attempt, she and fellow activist Cornelia Emilian founded the Women's League in Iaşi in 1894.

When the league folded five years later, Reuss-Ianculescu moved to Bucharest. She had some success as a writer, publishing several novels including *Towards Emancipation* in 1903 and *Woman's Fate* in 1906. As her profile rose, she gave a series of lectures on women's rights at the Romanian Athenaeum in Bucharest.

In 1901 Reuss Ianculescu founded the Women's Emancipation Society, later renamed the League for Romanian Women's Rights and Duties. It was the first association in Romania specifically aiming to obtain the vote for women.

One of her strategies was to include influential men in the league's leadership in a bid to gain leverage with politicians; she also believed that men and women had complementary abilities that could be usefully combined.

The league lobbied the parliament to incorporate women's suffrage into the new Romanian constitution, but despite her efforts and those of other feminists, women were treated as legal incompetents in the 1923 constitution. Women finally gained the right to vote in local elections in 1929 and in general elections in 1938, a few months before Reuss-Ianculescu died. However, they were stripped of this right the following year, only re-gaining the right to vote in 1946.

PROFILE: ELENA CEAUSESCU

Elena Ceauşescu was born Lenuţa Petrescu into a peasant family 1916, though she later claimed to have been born in 1919 so she would appear to be younger than her husband, the communist dictator Nicolae Ceauşescu.

After moving to Bucharest and working in a textile factory, she joined the Romanian Communist Party where she met Ceauşescu. The two married in December 1947.

Initially, Elena Ceauşescu was a secretary in the foreign ministry in Romania's first communist government; it was only after her husband became general secretary of the party that she took senior positions in the Romanian Communist Party.

In 1973 she was appointed to the Politburo, and was considered the most influential person in the country after her husband. Both Ceauşescus were the centre of a personality cult, with Elena styled "Mother of the Nation".

However, the communist regime came crashing down in December 1989 when protests that started in Timisoara spread across the country, erupting into revolution. The Ceauşescus fled Bucharest, but were captured in the nearby town of Targoviste. On 25 December 1989, they were executed by firing squad.

Elena Ceauşescu is reported to have screamed "You motherf*****s!" as she was put up against the wall, while here husband sang the *Internationale*.

Controversy later emerged about Elena Ceauşescu's academic record. Although she left school at 14, she allegedly graduated from the University of Bucharest with a PhD in polymer chemistry, but after her death and the collapse of communism several Romanian scientists claimed they had been forced to write academic papers in her name.

POLITICS

Romania is a semi-presidential democracy. The president is directly elected, and can serve a maximum of two five-year terms. Members of the two houses of parliament - the chamber of deputies and the senate - are elected for four-year terms.

Romania's incumbent President is Klaus Iohannis, the former mayor of the Transylvanian city of Sibiu. He was elected in 2014 with the support of the centre-right National Liberal Party (PNL).

The December 2016 general election delivered a majority for the PNL's arch-rival, the centre-left Social Democratic Party (PSD), setting up an uneasy cohabitation between Iohannis and the PSD and its coalition partner the Alliance of Liberals and Democrats (ALDE).

The PNL performed poorly in the election, losing votes to the PSD and to a new centre-right party, the Union Save Romania (USR), which ran on an anti-corruption platform.

Romania has been largely exempt from the wave of populism and "illiberal democracy" that has been on the rise in Hungary and Poland. All the main parties represented in the parliament are in favour of EU membership and want Romania to adopt the euro.

Corruption is currently the hottest issue in Romanian politics. An attempt by the PSD to water down anti-corruption legislation by government decree failed in early 2017, after mass protests forced the government to scrap the decree. At their peak on February 5, over half a million Romanians demonstrated against the government in Bucharest and other cities.

PROFILE: LAURA CODRUTA KOVESI

Laura Codruţa Kovesi is arguably the most powerful woman in Romania. Admired by both the international community and many ordinary Romanians who applaud her success in pursuing high-level corruption cases, she is feared and hated by many politicians.

Kovesi was appointed chief prosecutor of the National Anticorruption Directorate (DNA) in 2013. She was previously the Prosecutor General of Romania attached to the High Court of Cassation and Justice, a position she took up in 2006 at the age of just 33.

Under Kovesi's leadership, the DNA has been highly active in bringing senior politicians and businesspeople suspected of corruption to account. They include Romania's sitting Prime Minister Victor Ponta, who came under investigation on 17 separate charges of forgery, money laundering and tax evasion in July 2015, before stepping down four months later. The DNA has also probed Bucharest mayor Sorin Oprescu, Finance Minister Darius Valcov and hundreds of others including ministers, MPs, mayors and local and national government officials.

Personally, interviewers such as The Guardian in 2015 have described Kovesi as "quiet [and] unassuming", with some describing the religious icons on the walls of her simple office. A recent poll showed that 60% of Romanians trust the DNA compared to a trust rating of just 11% for the parliament.

This sentiment is not shared by politicians, many of whom fear they or their associates will be the next to be targeted by the DNA. The parliament has frequently blocked investigations into its members, and Kovesi has come under fire for the organisation's cooperation with the secret services.

However, the attempt by the current government to undermine the DNA by partly decriminalising abuse of office - a move that was later reversed - outraged many Romanians, hundreds of thousands of whom turned out to demonstrate.

PROFILE: GABRIELA FIREA

Former journalist Gabriela Firea became Bucharest's first female mayor in June 2016.

Originally from the northeastern city of Bacau, she worked as a journalist and news presenter before being elected to the senate in 2012 on the ticket of the Social Democratic Party (PSD).

She is also the author of a book of poems, a novel and a children's book, and she has recorded an album of Moldovan folk music.

Her first husband, Răsvan Firea, died in 2010. The following year, she married Florentin Pandele, the mayor of Voluntari near Bucharest.

She memorably clashed with Romania's outspoken former President Traian Basescu, who called her "a good journalist, but is catastrophic as a lawyer". Firea filed a complaint against Basescu, accusing him of threats and extortion.

In 2014 Firea was appointed spokesman for the PSD, working directly with its leader, the country's then Prime Minister Victor Ponta.

Two years later, she stood in the Bucharest mayoral elections. Bucharest normally votes centre-right but the corruption probe launched into former mayor Sorin Oprescu in 2015 threw the race wide open. Changes to the voting procedure, which scrapped the second ballot, also favoured Firea since usually backers of other parties come together to defeat the PSD candidate in the second round.

As a result, Firea was elected mayor of Bucharest in June 2016, after taking 43% of the vote.

ECONOMY

Romania is currently one of the fastest growing economies in Europe, with the European Commission forecasting growth of 3.7% in 2017.

The recent surge in growth has been spurred on by policies such as slashing VAT, raising public sector wages and lowering social security contributions. This has resulted in a consumer boom in the last couple of years, with retail sales soaring, which has in turned resulted in a hike in imports as local manufacturers fail to keep pace with demand for consumer goods.

Critics including the International Monetary Fund (IMF) have warned that Bucharest is risking fiscal stability by pursuing expansionary fiscal policies - many of them promised in advance of the December 2016 general election. They argue that Bucharest should take advantage of the current rapid growth to invest into infrastructure; most investors in the country criticise Romania's poor road infrastructure and slow trains.

Despite these constraints, Romania's skilled workforce, low labour costs and proximity to Germany and other West European countries have helped the manufacturing sector to thrive, especially auto-components companies. Major companies include automakers Dacia (owned by Renault) and Ford Craiova, as well as auto components suppliers such as Continental, Dräxlmaier and Leoni. Many companies set up operations in Transylvanian cities such as Arad and Timisoara that are closer to Hungary's excellent road network.

The IT services sector is also booming, with international companies including Microsoft and Oracle setting up in Romania. As a result, competition for IT specialists is increasingly intense. In addition to Bucharest, the university towns of Cluj and Iasi have emerged as centres for the IT industry.

Romania's other advantages include more than 10mn hectares of agricultural land. It has one of the largest agricultural sectors in Europe in terms of the number of people employed - about 29% of the population - and agriculture contributes around 8% of GDP.

Once Europe's largest oil producer, Romania is now a net importer of oil and gas as a lot of its resources were used up during the communist era. However, the discovery of the offshore Domino gas field could change that when commercial production starts around 2020. Romania also has resources of coal, iron ore, copper, uranium, gold and other minerals.

A large amount of Romania's electricity comes from hydropower, with the Cernavoda Nuclear Power Plant also making a substantial contribution. Plans to build a second nuclear power plant have been under discussion for years. There has recently been a substantial effort to invest into renewable energy, though subsidies were later cut, leaving investors struggling.

Romania's real estate market experienced a boom in the run up to the country's EU accession in 2007, with many EU citizens - including from the UK - snapping up properties along the Black Sea coast. This bubble burst with the start of the international economic crisis in 2008. House and apartment prices are still well below 2008 levels, though they appeared to bottom out in 2012 and are now rising modestly.

Despite the recent growth, almost a decade after joining the EU, Romania remains one of the bloc's poorest countries - with only neighbouring Bulgaria having a lower GDP per capita. Romania has also struggled to benefit from EU structural funds, failing to use its full allocation in the 2007-2014 programme period, not least because planned infrastructure investment projects have been held back by corruption.

Nonetheless, given Romania's large population, the country has the potential to quadruple the size of its economy in the next two decades, raising it from 17th the largest EU economy to among the top 10, according to the Foreign Investors Council (FIC), which represents major investors in Romania. This would require hiking GDP to €655bn in 2036.

To meet this goal, numerous issues need to be resolved, not least stemming the tide of migration, as many Romanians continue to look for better opportunities abroad especially in fellow EU countries such as Spain and Italy. Romania's population has declined by around 4m since 1990, to just under 20m.

ARCHITECTURE

Most of Bucharest's buildings date back to the 19th century or later; almost nothing remains of the old Ottoman era city.

The achievement of independence in the mid 19th century resulted in an explosion of cultural expression and modernisation, including in architecture. Romania looked west, initially importing the romantic and neoclassical styles. But Romania also developed its own unique Neo-Romanian style, pioneered by Ion Mincu, the founder of the Romanian school of architecture.

This gave way in the early 20th century to the Symbolist style, bringing Art Deco to Romania. Many buildings from the 1920s and 30s incorporate motifs such as round windows reminiscent of the portholes on the ocean-going liners of that period. This contrasted with the Functionalist style that also emerged in the inter-war period with examples including the Gara de Nord, Bucharest's main railway station.

Another dramatic change came under the communist regime established after the Second World War. Nicolae Ceausescu's systemisation drive, which saw thousands of rural families forced out of their homes and into bleak new apartment blocks, was inspired by his visits to China and North Korea. Old districts were bulldozed to make way for high-density dormitory districts of uniform eight and ten story apartment blocks.

It was only the fall of communism in 1989 that prevented the city's historic heart - the Lipscani district - from being demolished. Nearby districts like Uranus, knocked down to make way for the gigantic Palace of the Parliament, were less fortunate.

In the two and a half decades since the fall of communism many modern glass and steel structures have been erected, especially in the central business district and to the north of the city.

Meanwhile, many of the city's older buildings have not fared well. A stroll through the Lipscani district or other older parts of the city reveals numerous signs saying "Cade tenicula" ("plaster falling"). Some are shored up with wooden scaffolds; others have plastic tape cordoning off the pavement in front to protect passersby from falling debris. These are the hundreds - possibly thousands - of neglected buildings that have heritage enthusiasts in Bucharest wringing their hands.

From palaces to former industrial buildings, the law says that buildings deemed to be of "historic interest" cannot be knocked down. Instead their owners, who either can't afford to rehabilitate them or want to make a profit from the land, leave them to rot. Some, allegedly, hasten their demise by damaging the roofs, letting in squatters and or lighting fires.

Such is the extent of the problem that in 2015, the World Monument Fund (WMF) added Bucharest to its list of 50 global sites at risk. Bucharest "is threatened by abandonment and demolition of historic buildings, uncontrolled development, and inappropriate rehabilitation," the fund said.

"Many factors now threaten the preservation of the surviving urban heritage," the fund's report explains. "Ownership disputes have arisen in the process of reversing the nationalisation of private properties. The court system's long delays in resolving them mean that many older buildings stay shuttered and neglected in the interim. At the same time, a growing economy has raised land values in the city centre, providing a strong incentive for demolition and redevelopment."

It's not only residential buildings that are at risk. Bucharest's oldest industrial building, the Assan Mill, has been damaged by fires several times, and is now barely standing. Attempts to rebuild it have failed, as its owners want to develop the land. Many other relicts of old industrial Bucharest have already disappeared.

However, it's not always a sad story. The former commodities exchange, built in 1898, also fell victim to fire and was abandoned by many years. However, it was taken over and has now been converted in into an office and event space - The Ark. Meanwhile, the old Cartea Romaneasca printing press is now an office centre with high profile clients like the European Bank for Reconstruction and Development(EBRD). Downstairs is an exhibition space and the Readers Cafe.

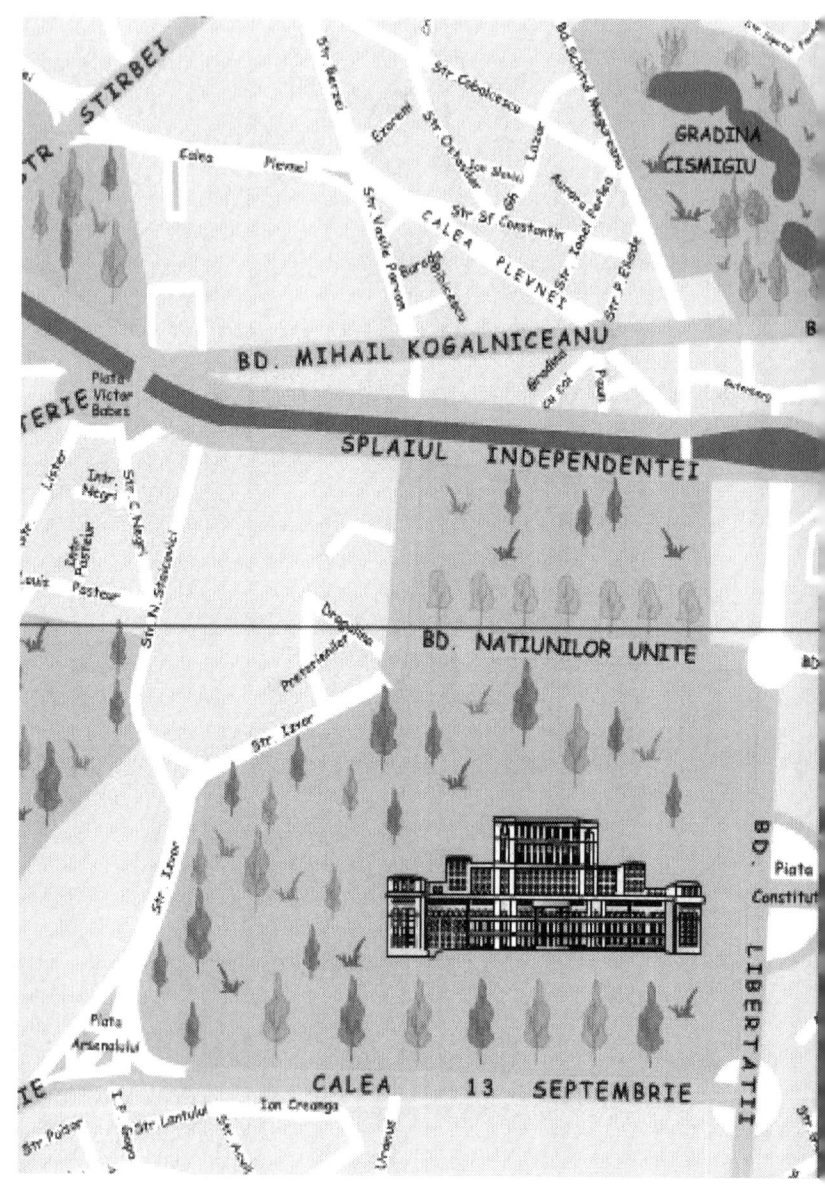

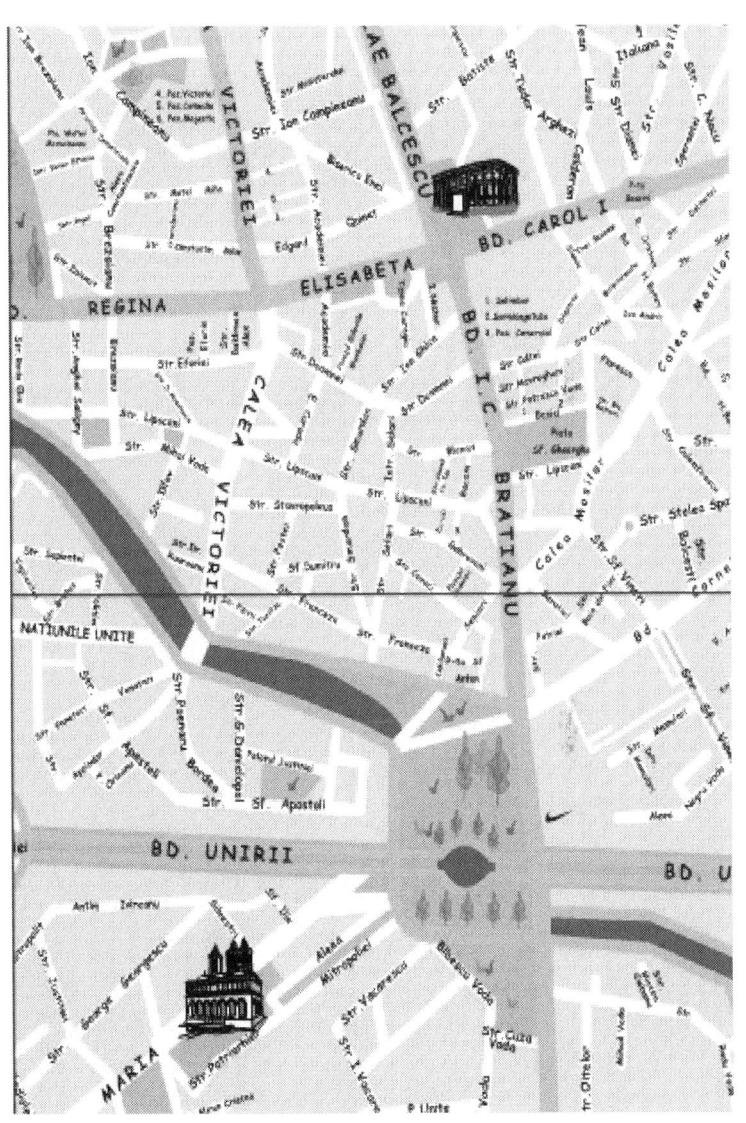

THE SINGLE GIRL'S GUIDE TO BUCHAREST

INSIDER Q&A WITH TOUR GUIDE ANA-MARIA
ADAMOAE

Single Girl's Guide to Bucharest: If you were describing Bucharest to someone who had never been there, what words would you use?

Ana-Maria Adamoae: A colourful puzzle that requires some effort to be solved. Think of Bucharest as Cinderella and you'll grow into loving it as you scratch beneath the surface to learn its stories. Bucharest might not be love at first sight, but for sure it's not a city to forget.

SGG2B: What are your top recommendations for places to go to get a feel for the city?

A-MA: A walk on Calea Victoriei, which is one of Bucharest's oldest and most famous streets, will be the perfect way to immerse yourself into the city's Golden Age. Here you can admire former private houses built by the wealthiest noble families starting mid-19th century, the former Royal Palace, the Romanian Athenaeum - the most famous concert hall in the country - and the oldest pastry shop in town still running on the ground floor of Capsa Hotel.

The dramatic recent past of Bucharest will unfold its stories while you walk along Unirii Boulevard, guarded by the enormous building used today by the parliament. An entire quarter was swiped off just to please our last communist dictator, Nicolae Ceausescu.

SGG2b: Where is the best place to spend a lazy Sunday afternoon in Bucharest?

A-MA: Unless you plan a winter trip, Bucharest has amazing tea or coffee houses hosted in charming old houses with lush green gardens. Infinitea, OAR Garden,

Dianei 4, Lente and Shift Pub are just some of the most popular places in town, and lots of locals love to spend a lazy afternoon or evening there.

Last but not least, fair weather is perfect for spending some time outdoors in one of Bucharest's parks, and if you want also to visit a unique museum I warmly recommend Herastrau Park, where we also have the Village Museum.

SGG2B: Do you have any special advice for women travelling alone?

A-MA: I don't have special advice, just to pay attention to the same things they do when travelling anywhere alone. Bucharest is just like any other European capital.

SGG2B: A big question for solo travellers is where they can feel comfortable dining alone. Would you recommend any cafes or restaurants?

A-MA: I usually recommend places where I love to go with my friends and family, but also by myself : Primus Pub, Manuc's Restaurant, Hanul Berarilor Casa Soare, La Mama (different locations through the city centre), Vatra and Journey's Pub. The food is delicious, the venues are centrally located and customers are both locals and tourists. They all have Facebook pages and websites in English as well.

SGG2B: What do you love most about Bucharest?

A-MA: Tough question... Its unique style, I suppose. I love that you never know what you'll find at the next corner, it's like a huge surprise gift wrapped in tons of layers.

SGG2B: Where are the best places to go for a day trip or weekend break outside Bucharest?

A-MA: Nestled in the foothills of the Carpathian mountains in the southeastern corner of Transylvania, Brasov is a picturesque medieval town where you can have a lovely day trip or a full weekend. On your way to Brasov, stop in Sinaia to visit Peles, an exquisite late 19th century castle where our first king spent his summers. While in Brasov, take a tour of the old fortifications, visit the Black Church and enjoy a coffee in the old square. A trip to Poienari, where Vlad the Impaler's real fortress was built on top of a mountain, combined with a scenic drive on the Transfagarasan highway - named by Top Gear as one of the most beautiful and dangerous roads in the world - is the perfect choice for the long summer days.

Ana-Maria Adamoae is a licensed tour guide who describes herself as madly in love with Bucharest. Find out more about her tailor-made tours at https://guidedtoursbucharest.wordpress.com, or contact Ana-Maria at aadamoae@gmail.com or 0729 729 682.

TOP SIGHTS

PALACE OF THE PARLIAMENT

A whole district of Bucharest was razed to make way for the Palace of the Parliament. The colossal palace is the fourth largest building in the world, and the second largest administrative building after the Pentagon. It also has the distinction of being the heaviest building in the world at just over 4bn kilos.

As well as Romania's two houses of parliament - the chamber of deputies and the senate - it also hosts the National Museum of Contemporary Art, the Museum of Communist Totalitarianism and the Museum of the Palace. Even so, much of the building is empty.

The palace was originally the piece de resistance of Communist dictator Nicolae Ceausescu's reconstruction plan for the city after the 1977 earthquake. Inspired by the North Korean capital Pyongyang, Project Bucharest was launched the following year, although construction of the palace only started in June 1984. Ceausescu never saw the completed palace, as he was executed in 1989.

The building was almost entirely built from Romanian materials, including 3,500 tonnes of crystal, 900,000 m3 of wood parquet and wainscotting and 200,000 m2 of woollen carpets.

Visits to the palace are by guided tour only, and a passport is needed for admittance to the building. Admission costs RON35 per person for a standard tour.

Address: 2-4, Izvor Street
tel: 0733 558 102, 0733 558 103; website: http://cic.cdep.ro/en/visiting/opening-hours-and-tariffs;
email: cic.vizite@cdep.ro
Opening hours: March-October, daily 09:00-17:00;
November-February, daily 10:00-16:00

VILLAGE MUSEUM

Cottages, mills and churches were transported from all over Romania to this huge outdoor museum near Herastrau Park. The oldest of the houses dates from the late 18th century, though most are from the mid 19th. Plaques by each building explain where they are from and there is also an audio commentary. The painted icons of the Dragomireşti church are particularly worth seeing.

The idea of an outdoor museum was first broached back in 1867, but the museum finally opened in 1936. During the second world war, families from the Bukovina region, which was occupied by Soviet forces, were housed in the museum.

The museum has three entrances, at 28 Kiseleff Avenue, 30 Kiseleff Avenue and the Miorita fate to Herastrau Park.
tel: 021 317 9103; email: contact@muzeul-satului.ro;
website: www.muzeul-satului.ro
Opening hours: Kiseleff Avenue Mon 9.00-17.00, Tues-Sun 9.00-19.00; Miorita gate Wed-Sun 11.00 - 19.00

PALATUL PRIMAVERII

This recently opened museum is the former home of Romania's communist era dictator Nicolae Ceausescu and his wife Elena. It provides fascinating insights into the lavish lifestyle of the country's first couple at a time when most Romanians were struggling to survive - evident from the indoor swimming pool, cinema and enormous wardrobes of the Ceausescus. The one hour tour of the palace has to be booked in advance.

Bulevardul Primaverii 50
tel: 021 318 0989; email: office@palatulprimaverii.ro;
website: www.palatulprimaverii.ro
Opening hours: Wed-Sun 10.00-18.00

CURTEA VECHE

The Old Princely Court was built in 1459, during the reign of Vlad III Dracula, though it has been rebuilt several times since then. Archaeological excavations were launched in 1953, and numerous artefacts are now on show in the museum. It is currently closed for renovation, with no news on the date of reopening, but much of the display can be seen from outside.

27-31 Franceza Street
tel: 0213 140 375

COTROCENI PALACE AND NATIONAL MUSEUM

The residence of Romania's president is open to the public though visits have to be booked in advance. Originally built by Serban Cantacuzino in 1678, the palace is an eclectic mix of styles including French and German. Remember to bring your ID.

Bulevard Geniului 1
tel: 021 221 1200; email: vizitare@muzeulcotroceni.ro;
website: http://www.muzeulcotroceni.ro/old/engleza/
vizitare_eng.html
Opening hours: Tues-Sun 09.30-17.30

PEASANT MUSEUM

This neo-Romanian redbrick building houses an extensive collection of over 100,000 items, including costumes and icons, tracing the history of Romanian peasant life. The home of peasant Antonie Mogos, which has been moved inside the building, is particularly worth seeing.

The museum was founded in 1906, but between 1948 and 1989 the building became Romania's communist party museum; the collectivisation exhibition still exists but has been removed to the basement. After the fall of communism the museum was revamped to become the Peasant Museum, and won the European Museum of the Year award back in 1996.

The museum is currently closed for renovation, although both the shop and some of the temporary galleries are still open.

Șoseaua Kiseleff 3
tel: 021 317 96 61; email: info@muzeultaranuluiroman.ro; website: www.muzeultaranuluiroman.ro
Opening hours: Tues-Sun 10.00-18.00, last entry 17.00

GEORGE ENESCU MUSEUM

Worth visiting just to get a look at the inside of the stunning Art Nouveau Cantacuzino Palace, one the most beautiful buildings in Bucharest. It is devoted to George Enescu (1881-1955), Romania's most famous musician, composer and conductor. Enescu was a child prodigy who started playing the violin at the age of four and composing a year later.

Enescu actually lived in a smaller house behind the place with his wife Maria Maruca Rosetti-Tescanu, the widow of the palace's original owner Mihail Cantacuzino. The house, which has the original furniture and fittings, is also open to the public.

Calea Victoriei 141
tel: 021 318 1450; email: office@georgeenescu.ro; website: www.georgeenescu.ro
Opening Hours: Tues-Sun 10.00-17.00, last admission 16.30

NATIONAL MUSEUM OF ART OF ROMANIA

The gallery is located in Romania's former royal palace, which suffered a devastating fire in 1926 and was again damaged in the 1989 revolution, but has since been rebuilt. As well as an extensive medieval collection, the gallery also houses collections of modern Romanian art including sculptures by Constantin Brâncuşi and paintings by Theodor Pallady and Gheorghe Petraşcu. The European Art Gallery, hosted in the palace's side wings, has Romania's largest collection of European art, much of it originally acquired by King Carol 1.

Opening hours: Wed-Sun 11.00 to 19.00 (May - September); Wed-Sun 10.00 to 18.00 (October – April). Calea Victoriei 49
tel: 021 313 3030; email: programari@art.museum.ro; website: www.mnar.arts.ro

PLUMBUITA MONASTERY

An oasis of calm in Plumbuita park, one of the huge lakeside parks in the north of the city along the Colentina river. The redbrick monastery is dedicated to the Nativity of St. John the Baptist, and it was first consecrated in 1560 though it has been rebuilt since then. It was given the name Plumbuita, which translates roughly as "Leaded" when it was covered in lead sheets. Legend has it that the Wallachian prince Matei Basarab ordered the lead to be melted to make cannon balls when he ran short of ammunition mid battle. The monastery is also the site of Bucharest's first printing press, established in 1573, and there is a small library and museum with several 500 year old books. The monastery is currently undergoing renovation.

Str. Plumbuita 58
tel:: 021 242 1728; email: manastireaplumbuita@yahoo.com; website: www.manastirea-plumbuita.ro

A STROLL ALONG THE CALEA VICTORIEI

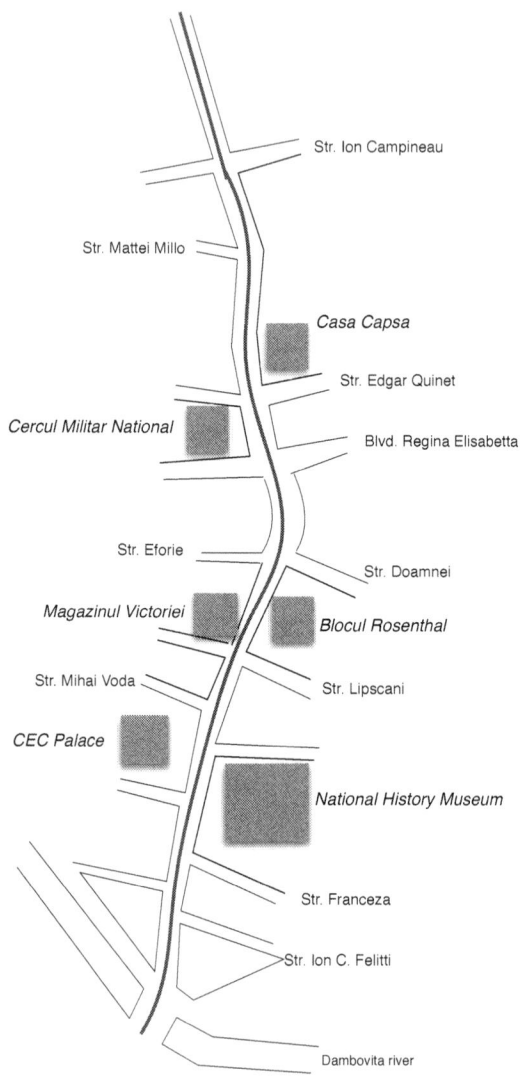

Str. Ion Campineau

Str. Mattei Millo

Casa Capsa

Str. Edgar Quinet

Cercul Militar National

Blvd. Regina Elisabetta

Str. Eforie

Str. Doamnei

Magazinul Victoriei

Blocul Rosenthal

Str. Mihai Voda

Str. Lipscani

CEC Palace

National History Museum

Str. Franceza

Str. Ion C. Felitti

Dambovita river

A stroll along the Calea Victoriei (Victory Street) means taking a walk through the history of Bucharest. It has been the capital's most fashionable street for centuries under a variety of names, gaining its current title in 1878 after victorious Romanian armies returned down the street fresh from battles against Romania's Ottoman rulers.

Start the walk at the bottom of the Calea Victoriei, where it meets the Dambovita river, diagonally across from the rather grand Bucharest court of appeal.

The very first building on the right is one of the street's many palaces, now looking very grimy and sorry for itself, with a ragged looking EU flag outside fluttering outside.

Here, the Calea Victoriei skirts the old town. The first street on the right, into the old town, is unloved and shabby too, with many boarded up windows - completely unlike the renovated streets further along with their bustling cafes and restaurants.The street is named after Ion Filitti, a historian and diplomat who secretly opposed joining the tripe Entente in the First World War. To the left is Forza Rossa, the Ferrari owners' club of Bucharest.

Further along to the right is the National History Museum, the first really important landmark. At the weekend there's usually at least one wedding party getting photographed here, and probably a group of schoolchildren too.

The museum used to be the Postal Services Palace, built back in 1892, and modelled on the Geneva post office. The large rectangular building has a portico at the front, supported by 10 Doric columns

Opposite is one of the most dramatic contrasts of the Calea Victoriei. The gorgeous CEC Palace hosts Romania's oldest bank Casa de Economii și Consemnațiuni (CEC). The palace was built on the site of a former monastery, which fell into ruins and was knocked down in 1875. 25 years later, the CEC Palace was opened.

Right next door to the CEC palace is the brand new plate glass headquarters of Romania's largest bank BCR, which is owned by Austria's Erste bank. You can see the old glass and metal dome of the CEC Palace reflected in the walls of BCR.

The small Zlatari Church on the right is known as the church where miracles come true. It hosts the right hand of Saint Cyprian of Antiochia, who legend has it was a wizard. He later converted to Christianity and died as a martyr. He is believed to have the power to defend people against spells and wizards - probably the reason this church often has a queue waiting outside! The original 17th century church was damaged by earthquakes in the early 19th century and the current church was started in 1850.

Next comes the fork-shaped Pasajul Macca-Vilacrosse, a glassed in arcade leading off the Calea Victoriei into the old town. The site of an old inn, in the 19th century it was replaced by the current two story buildings, with the small passages - Vilacrosse and Macca leading between them. The passage initially housed Bucharest's first Stock Exchange, then jewellery shops, and is now mainly populated by bars and restaurants.

The busy Regina Elizabetta street intersects Calea Victoriei here, close to the university district.

Immediately after Regina Elizabetta street on your left is the Cercul Militar Naţional, also known as the Officers' Circle Palace, with its name etched on its neo-classical facade. It was built on the site of the old Sărindar monastery for the officers of the Bucharest military garrison. The restaurant and the terrace are open to the public. The 1960s building opposite was designated for military officers.

Cafe Capsa on your right is one of Bucharest's oldest cafes, opened in 1852. While it's generally fairly quiet now, it featured in Olivia Manning's Fortunes of War as a popular hangout for locals at the beginning of the second world war. The interior reflects its history, with chandeliers and baroque furnishings.

The management claims this was once the finest pastry shop in Europe, selling mainly oriental confectionery, although in the second half of the 19th century it introduced the western delights of lemonade, cakes, bonbons and chocolates, often imported from Paris.

Yet another variation on the palace, this time the art deco Bucharest Telephone Palace, now owned by Telekom Romania. At 52.5 metres high, this was the tallest building in Bucharest until the 1950s.

The project was launched by the American trust Morgan, one of the predecessors of giant financial services firm JP Morgan Chase & Co, which got a 20-year monopoly on Romanian telephone services in return for issuing a loan to Bucharest after the 1929 Wall Street Crash hit the Romanian economy.

A major reconstruction project was launched in the 1990s, which included reinforcing the roof to bear microwave antennas and rebuilding the exterior. This became Romania's largest architectural reconstruction project.

Another intriguing reconstruction project is right next door, where the modern plate glass structure of the Novotel rises out of a replica of the old baroque facade of the National Theatre Bucharest. The theatre, which has also been immortalised on RON100 banknotes, was destroyed in the Luftwaffe's bombing of Bucharest in August 1944.

On the other side of the road a couple of passageways, Pasaj Victoriei and the English Pasaj lead through to Academy Street.

The English Pasaj is particularly notorious. When the building was bought by Grigore Eliade, who transformed it into the English Hotel in 1885, the passageway was built, modelled on the passages in fashionable West European capitals. Most of the hotel's rooms were located along the tall (several stories high) but narrow passage. However, the rooms were too small for the hotel to withstand competition from other newer hotels, and it was transformed into a luxury brothel. Customers reportedly included King Carol II.

The accommodation is now private housing - be discreet taking photos as the residents don't like it. It is poorly maintained, and many of the balconies where ladies of the night once advertised their wares look close to collapse.

Bucharest's designer heaven starts around here, with the Mingotti store followed by Emporio Armani and several high-end jewellery stores.

Cretzulescu Church, on the corner of Revolution Square, was commissioned in 1720–1722 by the boyar (aristocrat) Iordache Crețulescu and his wife Safta, one of the daughters of Wallachian prince Constantin Brâncoveanu.

The facade was originally painted, but has been redbrick since a restoration in the 1930s. The church was damaged in the earthquakes of 1940 and 1977, and the 1989 revolution, and narrowly escaped demolition in the early days of the communist regime.

In front of the church is a bust of politician Corneliu Coposu (1916-1995), who served 17 years in prison under the communist regime.

Revolution Square is the site of one of arguably the most significant moment in recent Romanian history, Ceausescu's final speech in December 1989.

As the uprising in the city of Timisoara threatened to spread across the country, the communist dictator decided to address the population in a televised speech from the balcony of the Central Committee building in what was then known as Piața Palatului, or Palace Square.

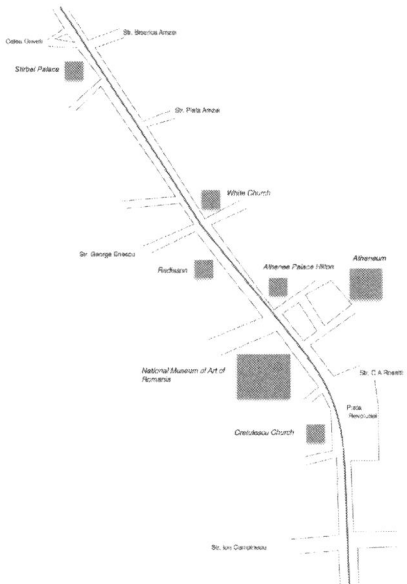

However, just minutes into the speech, the crowd started to chant "Ti-mi-șoa-ra! Ti-mi-șoa-ra!" Ceausescu's attempt to placate the crowd failed, and he was hustled off the balcony by security. The speech marked the beginning of the Romanian revolution that rapidly toppled Ceausescu and his regime.

The Central Committee building, which still houses government offices, dominates the right hand side of the square, which has since been renamed Piața Revoluției or Revolution Square.

Another monument to the revolution is the Memorial of Rebirth, a 25-metre-high marble pillar with a metal crown, rather like a tangled ball of wire, close to its peak. The €1.5mn monument was the source of controversy, and was criticised for failing to reflect the significance of the revolution. It has gained various mocking nicknames such as the "olive on a toothpick" and "the potato of the revolution". In 2012 bright red paint was spattered close to the top of the spike, and has never been removed.

The plaza surrounding the memorial is popular with skateboarders, even after it was surrounded by a display of spiky metal sculptures.

On the right hand side of the square is the former Royal Palace, which now houses the National Museum of Art of Romania.

Another significant building is the Romanian Athenaeum. The garden in front of the domed building is a popular place for families to sit in summer.

At the end of the square is the Athenee Palace Hilton, probably Bucharest's most famous hotel, and the site of many WW2 intrigue.

Further along the Calea Victoria is the White Church, with its beautifully restored interior.

About 100m further north on the left is the gracious but neglected Ştirbei Palace. The extensive garden behind the palace is home to Gradina Eden, one of Bucharest's most popular outdoor bars in summer.

Close to the Ştirbei Palace, one of the largest buildings on the Calea Victoriei is home to the Museum of Art Collections.

Step away from the noise and traffic of the Calea Victoriei for a few minutes in Nicolae Iorga, a pleasant green space named after the historian, politician and playwright.

Close by is the Casino Palace in the historic Casa Vernescu, one of the showiest of the 19th century palaces built along this street. After the fall of communism, it was the subject of an acrimonious ownership dispute.

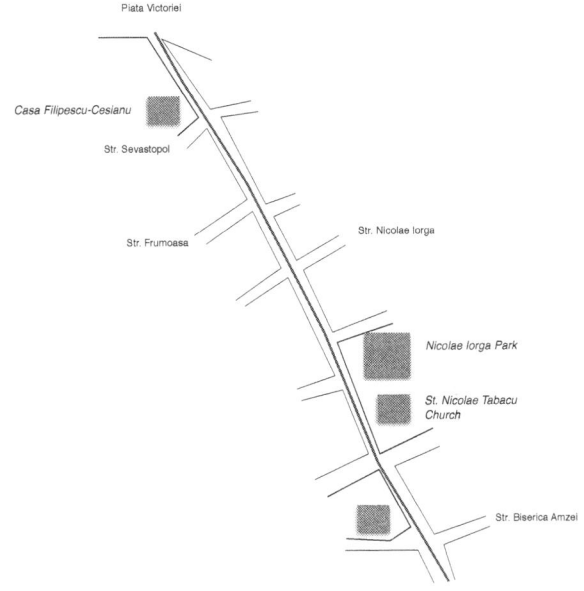

Piata Victoriei

Casa Filipescu-Cesianu

Str. Sevastopol

Str. Frumoasa

Str. Nicolae Iorga

Nicolae Iorga Park

St. Nicolae Tabacu
Church

Str. Biserica Amzei

As you approach the end of the Calea Victoriei, the recently rehabilitated Casa Filipescu-Cesianu is the home to a newly opened museum, Muzeul Vârstelor or the Museum of the Ages, dedicated to urban anthropology.

The walk ends at the vast Piata Victoriei, the site of the mass protests in early 2017. An empty plinth at the entrance to the square has been daubed with the worlds "Monument to Corruption". On the right of the square are the main government offices, while to the north are the Peasant Museum and Natural History Museum.

MUSEUMS

GRIGORE ANTIPA NATIONAL HISTORY MUSEUM

Next door to the Peasant Museum, the Museum of Natural History was founded back in 1834, making it one of the oldest Romanian research institutions. It is named after Grigore Antipa (1867-1944), a naturalist and explorer from Iasi.

The displays, most involving taxidermied animals, are well lit and informative, and the new electronic displays have an English option.

Highlights include the giant mantis suspended above the stairwell and the skeleton of a hump-backed whale. As well as exhibits from Romania, there are also flora and fauna from as far away as the Arctic Ocean and Malaysia.

1 Sos. Kiseleff
tel: 021.312.88.26; website: www.antipa.ro
Opening hours: 1 April - 31 October: Tues-Sun
10.00-20.00; 1 November - 31 March: Tues-Fri
10.00-18.00, Sat-Sun 10.00-19.00

BUCHAREST MUNICIPALITY MUSEUM

Built in the 1830s, the Suțu Palace once hosted the first ball of every social season. Its impressive interior was designed by the sculptor Karl Storck. Since 1956 it has hosted the Bucharest Municipality Museum, with collections and exhibitions related to the history of the Romanian capital. It was reopened after a renovation in 2015.

Opening hours: Tues-Sun 10.00-18.00
Bulevardul Ion C. Brătianu 2
tel: 021 315 6858; website: www.muzeulbucurestiului.ro/
En/bucharest-municipality-museum---sutu-palace.html

JEWISH MUSEUM

The museum gives fascinating insights into the life of Jews in Romania through ages, and their relationship with the country's rulers. As well as the substantial library of books written or translated by Romanian Jews, there is also a collection of paintings, items from Jewish theatres and a display of anti-Semitic posters. A separate room hosts a small Holocaust memorial.

The museum is currently closed for renovation and will reopen in 2017.

Intrarea Mămulari 3
tel: 021 311 0870
Opening hours: Mon-Thurs 09.00-15.00, Fri-Sun 09.00-13.00

SIGHET MEMORIAL EXHIBITION

The Sighet Memorial Exhibition tells the stories of those who suffered under the communist regime. It's a smaller offshoot of the Sighet Memorial Museum in Maramures, which is housed in a former prison where each of the cells has a different theme. The exhibition is currently closed for renovation and is due to reopen in 2017.

Str. Jean Louis Calderon 66
www.memorialsighet.ro

NATIONAL MUSEUM OF AVIATION

Inside the museum is a overview of Romanian aviation, with information in English; outside a graveyard where decaying fighter jets, helicopters and radar equipment have been left to rust.

Str. Fabrica de Glucoza 2-4
tel: 021 232 0404

ADMIRAL VASILE URSEANU ASTRONOMICAL OBSERVATORY

Romania's first public observatory is located in a building strangely reminiscent of a ship. It was founded by Admiral Vasile Urseanu, a former naval officer with a passion for astronomy. The observatory is currently being renovated but astronomical observations are held in clear weather at Casei Filipescu-Cesianu (Calea Victoriei 151). Thurs-Sat 22.00; Wed & Sun 11.00-14.00.

21, Blvd. Lascăr Catargiu
tel: 021 2129644; email: dialog@astro-urseanu.ro;
website: www.astro-urseanu.ro

NATIONAL MILITARY MUSEUM

Romanian military history from the stone age to the present day. The museum offers interesting walk through Romanian history with some fine archeological finds as well as King Carol I's sword and King Ferdinand's Mannlicher pistol. There's also an outdoor display of tanks and military vehicles. Renovated in 2016.

Strada Mircea Vulcanescu 125-127
tel: 021 319 5904; email: relatii.publice@muzeulmilitar.ro;
website: http://smg.mapn.ro/muzeumilitar/index.html

MUSEUM OF THE NATIONAL BANK OF ROMANIA

This free tour would be worth taking just to see the stunning interior of the Romania central bank, an impressive white building on the edge of the old town, but it's also a fascinating history of the Romanian currency.

Visitors need to make an appointment before visiting by emailing muzeul@bnro.ro, with preferred date and time to visit, name, ID number and a phone number. Registration takes two working days to process.

8 Doamnei Street
email: muzeul@bnro.ro; website: http://www.bnr.ro/
Museum-of-the-National-Bank-of-Romania-2727.aspx
Opening hours: Mon-Fri 10.00-18.00, by appointment only. Tours start daily at 10.00, 12.00, 14.00 and 16.00.

CASA EXPERIMENTELOR

Recently opened science museum where visitors can take part in experiments during a one-hour tour.

Calea Vitan 242
Opening hours: July-September 10.00-21.00; October-June 09.00-20.00

tel: 031 101 2200, 0722 210 111; email:
office@casaexperimentelor.ro; website:
www.casaexperimentelor.ro

CFR MUSEUM

The history of railways in Romania, with a giant trainset - the biggest in Southeast Europe - taking up much of the display space.

Calea Grivitei 193 B
tel: 031 080 8610, 031 620 3902;
email: muzeu.cfr@cenafer.ro; website: https://
sites.google.com/site/cenaferwebsite/home/muzeu
Opening hours: Wed-Sun 10.00-16.00

NATIONAL MUSEUM OF OLD MAPS AND BOOKS

An extensive collection of old maps housed in a beautiful old building. The space dedicated to maps of the Balkans in the 17th to 19th centuries shows the shifting borders in this region.
Opening hours: Wed-Sun: 10.00-18.00
Str. Londra 39
email: office@muzeulhartilor.ro; website:
www.muzeulhartilor.ro

FOISORUL DE FOC

The old fire tower was the tallest building in Bucharest when it was built at the beginning of the 20th century, and there is still an impressive view from the top floor. The fire tower also contains an exhibition of firefighting with equipment and photos.

Boulevard Ferdinand I, 33
tel: 021 252 2884; email: contact@muzeulpompierilor.ro;
website: www.muzeulpompierilor.ro,
www.foisoruldefoc.ro
Opening hours: Mon-Fri 08.00-17.00

DIMITRIE LEONIDA TECHNICAL MUSEUM

Rather a hotchpotch of machinery ranging from cars to turbines to mining equipment in an industrial looking building at the entrance to Carol Park.

Str. General Candiano Popescu 2
tel: 021 336 9390; website: https://www.facebook.com/
pg/MuzeulTehnic/about/?ref=page_internal
Opening hours: Wed-Sun 10.30-18.00

MUSEUL SPORTULUI

Somewhat disappointing exhibition of medals, photos and sporting equipment inside this impressive curved building.

Bulevard Marasti 20A
tel: 021 796 1454; muzeul.sportului@mts.ro; website: www.muzeulsportuluiromania.ro
Opening hours: Mon-Fri 10.00-17.00, last entry 16.00; closed Sat-Sun but private visits possible by appointment.

MEMORIAL HOUSES

Several of Bucharest's artists, writers and scientists have been commemorated by turning their former homes into museums. From composer George Enescu to bacteriologist Victor Babes, visits to these memorial houses are a fascinating opportunity to see their homes, learn about their remarkable lives, examine their furniture, poke into their bathroom cabinets....

TUDOR ARGHEZI MEMORIAL HOUSE

Tudor Arghezi is Romania's best known 20th century poet, whose style melds traditional and modernist styles. His works also include novels, essays, journalism, translations and letters. The large (18 room) on Str. Mărţişor is where he lived from 1930 until his death in 1967.

Str. Mărţişor 26
Opening hours: Tues-Sun 09.00-17.00
tel: 021 332 5900

VICTOR BABES MUSEUM

Victor Babes was one of the founders of modern microbiology, who was one of the pioneers in the study of rabies, leprosy, diphtheria, tuberculosis and other infectious diseases, discovering more than 50 unknown germs. This small museum was set up by the scientist's son in his former home, the 1920s style house is located in an attractive part of Bucharest near Kiseleff Park.

Address: Str. Andrei Muresanu 14A
Opening hours: Wed-Sun 10.00-18.00
tel: 021 230 2302; website: www.muzeulbucurestiului.ro/muzeul-victor-babes.html

GEORGE SEVEREANU MUSEUM

The residence of the Bucharest Municiplaity Museum's first director, this museum hosts an impressive array of antiquities collected by radiologist Dr. George Severeanu from Romania, Bulgaria, Italy, and Greece. This was mainly funded by his wife Ana Severeanu, who inherited both the house and a large fortune. The Maria and Dr. George Severeanu collection was donated to the Bucharest Municipality Museum in 1939, but the residence was opened two decades later, in 1956. It also hosts temporary archeology exhibitions.

Address: Strada Henri Coandă 26
Opening hours: 10.00-18.00, guided tours by appointment only, email or call at least 48 hours in advance.
tel: 021 212 9648; email:
muzeul.severeanu@muzeulbucurestiului.ro; website:
muzeulbucurestiului.ro/En/george-severeanu--museum.html

THE NOTTARA MEMORIAL MUSEUM

Museum celebrating the world of actor C.I. Nottara and his son composer C.C. Nottara. This exhibition was until recently in the Nottara's former residence on Boulevard Dacia. However, the museum is currently being relocated and the new location and time of reopening is not clear.

ART GALLERIES

If you're into art, Bucharest has a huge amount to offer, from the huge state art museums to tiny contemporary galleries.

MUSEUM OF ART COLLECTIONS

Located in the Romanit Palace, which dates back to 1822, the permanent exhibition comprises a total of 44 collections donated to the Romanian state by local families. Much of the work is by late 19th and 20th century Romanian artists, though it also boasts one Van Gogh and several older stone carvings from Văcăreşti Monastery. The building itself is impressive. Romanian writer Ion Ghica extolled the stuccoed walls, thick carpets and Venetian crystal chandeliers. Two additional wings were added in the later 19th century when it became Romania's finance ministry.

Calea Victoriei 111
Opening hours: Wed-Sun 11.00 to 19.00 (May - September); Wed-Sun 10.00 to 18.00 (October – April). See website for evening openings.
website: http://www.mnar.arts.ro/en/museum-of-art-collections

Despite being housed in separate buildings, the Art Collections Museum, K.H. Zambaccian Museum and Theodor Pallady Museum are all officially part of the National Museum of Art of Romania (MNAR).

ZAMBACCIAN MUSEUM

The former house of businessman and art collector Krikor Zambaccian displays works by Romanian artists including Zambaccian's portrait by Corneliu Baba, as well as international works by artists including Picasso and French Impressionists.

Str. Muzeul Zambaccian 21 A
Opening hours: Wed-Sun 11.00 to 19.00 (May -
September); Wed-Sun 10.00 to 18.00 (October – April).
tel: 021 230 1920; website: http://www.mnar.arts.ro/en/
k-h-zambaccian-museum

THEODOR PALLADY MUSEUM

An extensive collection of paintings, prints and drawings
by by Theodor Pallady, donated to the Romanian state in
the 1960s, as well as European paintings and sculptures.
Opening hours: Wed-Sun 11.00 to 19.00 (May -
September); Wed-Sun 10.00 to 18.00 (October – April).
Str. Spătarului 22
tel: 021 211 4979; website: http://www.mnar.arts.ro/en/
theodor-pallady-museum

National Museum of Contemporary Art
An eclectic collection of Romanian and East European
contemporary work housed in a new wing of the Palace of
the Parliament. The museum also holds regular temporary
exhibitions.
Opening hours: Wed-Sun 10.00-18.00, closed on public
holidays.
Palace of the Parliament wing E4, Izvor Streer 2-4, access
through Calea 13 Septembrie
tel: 021 318 9137; email info@mnac.ro; website:
www.mnac.ro

KUBE MUSETTE

This tiny exhibition space is in an empty shop next door to
the iconic Musette shoe shop, and has a frequently
changing range of installations.

Calea Victoriei 114
website: https://www.facebook.com/KubeMusette/

THEODOR AMAN MUSEUM

The Theodor Aman Museum reopened in June 2016 after a sympathetic restoration. Painter Theodor Aman was instrumental in founding the first art galleries and art schools in Bucharest after returning from Paris to be shocked that Romania had no higher education art schools. His Belle Epoque home is one of the most beautiful private residences in Bucharest, and was opened back in 1908, making it one of the oldest museums in the capital. Among the paintings and heavy dark carved furniture, the painted frescoes in the entrance hall and reception room steal the show. Aman collaborated with sculptor Karl Storck on the interior.

Str. C.A. Rosetti 8
Opening hours: Wed-Sun 10:00-18:00.
tel: 021 314 5812; website: http://
www.muzeulbucurestiului.ro/muzeul-theodor-aman.html

FREDERIC AND CECILIA CUTESCU-STORCK ART MUSEUM

This modern art museum is in a building designed by artists Frederic Storck and Cecilia Cuțescu-Storck. Opened in 1951, it shows works by the four Storck artists as well as a collection of medieval religious sculptures.

Str. Vasile Alecsandri 16
Opening hours: Wed-Sun 10.00-18.00.
tel: 021 211 3889; website: http://muzeulbucurestiului.ro/
En/frederic-storck-and-cecilia-cutescu-stork--
museum.html

FUTURE MUSEUM

The Future Museum sets itself apart from the contemporary art scene in Bucharest.The museum's website says it "is not a part of the contemporary network ... whose aims are to turn art into a commodity revolving around profitable investment". Instead, the museum is described as "an open platform with a belief in unexplored concepts... the new altar of the future.*

Ion Ghica 11
Opening hours: Mon-Fri 08.00-16.30.
website: www.futuremuseum.ro

THE ART TOWER, PANTELIMON

Make a Point decided to turn the water tower at the old Postavaria Romana textiles factor into an exhibition space in 2012. Since then a spiral staircase has been built around the tower taking visitors to where the water tank is held 30 metreS above of the city.

Sos. Morarilor 1
Opening hours: Thurs 19.00-20.00, Sat-Sun 13.00-18.00, other times by appointment
website: www.makeapoint.ro

ATELIER 030202

The Atelier 030202 contemporary art space dedicated to young visual artists interested in experimental visual design and new media.

Sala Noua, Teatrului de Comedie, Str. Sfânta Vineri nr. 11
Opening Hours: Mon-Sun 10.00-18.00
http://atelier030202.blogspot.ro

THEATRE & MUSIC

ROMANIAN ATHENEUM

Completed in 1888, the Romanian Atheneum has become an architectural symbol of Romania. Over the last 130 years, musicians and orchestra have played, scientists and academics have lectured, and paintings and sculptures displayed. The acoustics created by the huge cupola give a unique sound to concerts here.

Funds to build the Atheneum were raised through a national lottery, with 500,000 each costing one Leu issued to the population. Natural scientist Constantin Esarcu kicked off the campaign, saying "Give one Leu for the Atheneu(m)!"

For programmes and tickets go to: http://fge.org.ro/en/tickets.html
Address: 1-3 Str. Franklin
Ticket Office: 021 315 6875

ROMANIAN NATIONAL OPERA

The Romanian National Opera in Bucharest was built in 1953, and the first opera performed there was Tchaikovsky's Queen of Spades early the following year. Today, the seasons runs from September to June. Some performances are held in the smallerYellow Foyer alongside the main auditorium.

Schedule: http://operanb.ro/calendar/
Bd. Mihail Kogălniceanu 70-72, sect. 5, Bucureşti, România
Telefon: +4021.314.69.80

NATIONAL THEATRE, BUCHAREST

The historic theatre was destroyed in the Second World War, and since the 1970s, the National Theatre has been in a modern building on Piaţa Universităţii. Recently rebuilt, it was reopened in late 2014, and with seven halls including the huge Grand Hall it is one of the biggest theatres in Europe.

Box office: http://www.tnb.ro/en/box-office
Address: Bd. Nicolae Bălcescu nr. 2
tel: 0314 71 71; email: tnbpress@yahoo.com

MIHAIL JORA CONCERT HALL

Also known as the Romanian radio hall, the Mihail Jora Concert Hall is Romania's largest concert hall for symphonic and choral concerts, and is considered to be the best in the capital for acoustics. It is the home of the Romanian Radio Orchestras and Choirs, which comprise seven musical ensembles. The hall was recently reopened after its first ever refurbishment.

http://en.orchestreradio.ro/
General Berthelot St, No. 60-64
tel: 021 303 1211, 021 303 1517; email:
orchestreleradio@gmail.com

NATIONAL OPERETTA THEATRE

The Operetta and Musical Theatre Ion Dacian is closed for renovation, but check their website for shows at other venues.

http://www.opereta.ro/

GREEN HOURS

One of the most popular venues for jazz in Bucharest, Green Hours cafe and bar is open 24 hours a day, while there is a full programme of jazz in the basement. It also hosts an annual jazz festival.

Calea Victoriei, nr. 120
http://greenhours.ro

TUNES PUB

Karaoke bar deep in the heart of the old town, with an extensive cocktail menu.

Address: Gabroveni Street, No. 16
Book a table: rezervari@tunes.ro
tel: 0740 883 252; email: rezervari@tunes.ro; website: http://tunes.ro

ACCOMMODATION

Price bands are based on the price per night for a single room in high season.

UNDER €40

LIAD HOTEL
Centrally located near University Square, the Lead Hotel is cheap with big air-conditioned rooms and helpful staff. Enjoy breakfast on the roof terrace in summer.
Strada Coltei nr. 44
tel: 0214 240 030, 0736 859 297; email: office@liadhotel.com; website: http://liadhotel.com/

HOTEL CARPATI IMPARATUL ROMANILOR
Excellent location close to Cismigiu Gardens, and recently renovated.
str. Matei Millo, nr. 16
tel: 021 315 0140; email: rezervari@hotelcarpatibucuresti.ro; website: http://bucuresti.imparatulromanilor.ro/

BUCHAREST BOUTIQUE ACCOMMODATION
The owner Bogdan offers great hospitality at this attractively furnished hotel in a residential district around 1km from the old town.
37 Vitejescu Street
tel: 0760 296 630; email: bucharestboutiqueaccommodation@gmail.com; website: http://bucharest-boutique-accommodation.ro/

CITY GARDEN HOTEL
Located in the Stefan cel Mare district to the north of the old town, this hotel is quiet, cozy and clean. There's a wellness area with a sauna and outdoor hot tub.
Str. Chile 4
tel : 0758 053 812; email: info@citygardenhotel.ro; website: http://www.citygardenhotel.ro/

€40-€80

ELYSIUMHOTEL APARTMENTS
Aparthotel Elysium provides elegant, modern apartments with a double bedroom, living room with a sofa bed and a fully equipped kitchen. The hotel is slightly to the north of the centre in a residential area, close to the Dinamo stadium. Stefan Cel Mare metro station is 500m away.
Str. Ion Bogdan 21
tel: 021 659 6743, 0786 722 355;
email: bookings@elysiumhotel.ro; website:
www.elysiumhotel.ro

HOTEL CAPITOL
Right on the edge of the old town near the lively University area, the Hotel Capitol has its own restaurant as well as the many dining options nearby. Staff are very helpful, though some of the rooms are a little noisy.
Calea Victoriei 29
tel: 021 315 80 30; website: www.hotelcapitol.ro

VILA PARLIAMENT SQUARE
Great value for money, the clean and modern Vila Parliament Square is 700m from the Palace of the Parliament. Rooms are air conditioned and some have balconies.
Str. Lantului, nr.3A
tel: 0744 402 402, 031 411 1333, 031 411 1999; email: contact@parliamentsquare.ro; website:
www.parliamentsquare.ro

GRAND BOUTIQUE HOTEL
An elegant boutique hotel right in the heart of Bucharest.
Str. Negustori, Nr. 1B
tel: 031 425 6230, 034 581 5256; email: rezervari@ grandboutiquehotel.ro; website: http:// grandboutiquehotel.ro/

OVER €80

REMBRANDT HOTEL
In the heart of the historic Lipscani district opposite the Romanian central bank, the 16 rooms of the funky Rembrandt Hotel have contemporary decor and huge beds, and are surprisingly quiet. Breakfast at Café Klein in the hotel is recommended.
Str. Smârdan 11
tel: 021 313 93 15; email: info@rembrandt.ro; website: www.rembrandt.ro

ATHENEE PALACE HILTON
The Athenee Palace Hilton needs a mention not just because of its popularity with guests but because of its colourful history. In the second world war, diplomats, spies and journalists rubbed shoulders in the English Bar, with exchanges between Axis and Allied guests becoming more heated as the war continued. Today the hotel offers complimentary access to a 24 hours fitness centre and several restaurants - Café Athénée, Roberto's, the La Strada terrace and of course the English Bar.
Strada Episcopiei 1-3
tel: 021 303 3777; email: reservations.bucharest@hilton.com; website: www.atheneepalace-hotel.ro

HOTEL CHRISTINA PLUS
Hotel Christina Plus is in northern Bucharest not far from Floreasca Park. Rooms have private spa baths and saunas.
43 Intrarea Tudor Ştefan
tel: 021 367 0217

EPOQUE HOTEL
In a quiet yet central location near Cismigiu Central Park, this elegant boutique hotel offers free access to its spa and small indoor swimming pool. Staff have a reputation for being helpful and friendly.
17C Intrarea Aurora
tel: 021 312 3232; email: reception@epoque.ro; website: www.hotelepoque.ro

HOTEL CISMIGIU

In a recently renovated historic building, the Cismigiu is close to both Cismigiu Park and the old town - the modern interior contrasts pleasingly with the historic outside. Several of the modern suites have a fully equipped kitchen.
38 Regina Elisabeta Boulevard
tel: 0314 030 500; email: reservations@hotelcismigiu.ro;
website: www.hotelcismigiu.ro

HOSTELS

ANTIQUE HOSTEL

Highly recommended by backpackers, the Antique Hostel is centrally located and has a fully equipped kitchen, washing machine and yard with barbecue.
Splaiul Independentei 2A
tel: 031 425 8519; website: www.antiquehostel.ro

UMBRELLA HOSTEL

In a renovated 1920s building, Umbrella Hostel is 350m from Piaţa Romană Metro station. The hostel has large simply furnished rooms, some with private bathrooms. There's a bar and terrace, and the kitchen is clean and spacious.
Str. General Christian Tell Street 21
tel: 021 212 50 51; email:
booking@umbrellahostel.com; website:
umbrellahostel.com

EATING AND DRINKING

Dividing Bucharest's venues into cafes, bars and restaurants can be tricky. It's not uncommon to find a laid back cafe by day that turns into a buzzing bar through the evening into the small hours. Many of these cafe-cum-bars also serve food, blurring the lines still further.

These bars/cafes are often the best option for dining solo or having a quiet early evening drink. While we love characterful restaurants like Caru cu Bere, sadly they are more geared to groups or couples when the evening gets going.

CAFES

Bucharest has more coffee shops than you can shake a biscotti at. Here are some that we like but we also recommend trying out your local neighbourhood coffee shop - chances are it will have excellent coffee and a strong WiFi signal.

BOUTIQUE DU PAIN
Popular with government workers from the nearby ministries, Boutique du Pain has a good selection of lunches and patisserie.
Strada Academiei 28-30

DIANEI 4
A cafe/restaurant in a historic house, with a great atmosphere.
Strada Dianei, Nr. 4

GRAND CAFE VAN GOGH
This lively cafe has an outdoor terrace facing the central bank in the heart of the old town. A wide range of food as well as coffee and cakes.
Str. Smârdan 9

INFINITEA
Elegantly retro, with a wide range of teas.
str. Dr. Grigore Romniceanu, nr.7

LA COFETARIE BY TORTURI DE VIS
An easy to overlook cafe on the ground floor of one of the
communist era blocks on Bulevard Unirii, the decor is
fairly basic but the cakes, coffees and smoothies are a
revelation. Service is among the best in town.
Bd Unirii nr. 17

LENTE
Lente means slowly in Romanian and this cafe is aptly
named. Located down an alley lined with outdoor tables
under vines in summer, it seems a world away from the
bustle of the old town and business districts
Strada Arcului 8

M60
Near the boho Amzei area, M60 is popular among local
artists and writers, some of whom use it as their unofficial
office. As well as excellent coffee, M60 has a range of light
lunches and tasty cakes. In summer, M60 also has an
outside venue on the corner of Calea Victoriei and Str.
Rosetti.
Str. Mendeleev 2

ORIGO
By general consensus, the best coffee in Bucharest. One of
the first specialty coffee shops to open in Bucharest, they
also roast their own beans and supply other cafes in the
city.
Str. Lipscani 9

PAUL
Can't go wrong with this international coffee and patisserie
chain. Locations include Promenada Mall and Boulevard
Magheru 28-30.

STEAM
A tiny coffee shop offering some of the best espresso in town.
Strada Uruguay 22

FOOD ON THE MOVE

SNACK ATTACK
Sandwiches, salads and drinks at four locations: City Gate North Tower, Piata Presei Libere 3-5; Splaiul Independentei 7; Calea Victoriei 224, Calea Victoriei 12 A.

SUPER FALAFEL
Big selection of falafels and other vegetarian fast food.
Bulevardul Nicolae Bălcescu 36

SOUP UP!
A tiny vegan cafe serving soups, salads and cake (try the raw brownies!), newly opened but already gathering an eager lunch crowd.
Str. Piata Amzei 7-9

It's not hard to find a takeaway coffee in Bucharest. Some reliably good places are 5 to Go, Paul's and French Bakery.

Mega Image, Carrefour and other big supermarkets have a range of sandwiches, packaged salads and other prepared foods. Some Mega Image stores even have hot soup to take away in winter.

Malls including Promenade, Liberty, Sun Plaza all have big food courts with a wide range of different cuisines aimed at hungry shoppers and office workers on their lunch breaks.

Most restaurants allow takeaways of the dishes on their menus, just ask for your food "a la pachete". Use the same phrase if you want a doggie bag for uneaten food.

RESTAURANTS

BECA'S KITCHEN
Beca personally presides over this small and intimate restaurant serving home cooked organic food - highly recommended!
Opening hours: Tues-Fri 18:00-22:00, Sat: 12:00-22:00. Closed Sun and Mon.
Str. Mihai Eminescu 80
tel: 0744 344 700, 0722 308 960; email: home@becaskitchen.ro; website: www.becaskitchen.ro

BIUTIFUL
Stunning lakeside restaurant, open only during the summer. Their website specifies a smart-casual dress code.
Nordului Street 7-9
tel: 0733 500 222; email: officebythelake@biutiful.ro; website: http://bythelake.biutiful.ro/
Opening hours: Mon 15.00-02.00, Tues-Sun 12:00-02.00

CARU CU BERE
Located on historic Stavropoleos street, Caru cu Bere is a Bucharest institution. Visit for authentic Romanian food served by waitresses in flammable looking traditional costumes. There are floorshows in the usually packed restaurant during the evening. Get there early in summer if you want a seat on the terrace because it's only possible to book inside.
Opening hours: 08.00-00.00
Strada Stavropoleos 5
tel: 021 313 75.60, 0726 282 373; email: rezervari@carucubere.ro; website: www.carucubere.ro

GRADINA VERONA
This outdoor garden restaurant has a limited but tasty range of dishes.
Opening hours: 09.00-00.00
Strada Pictor Arthur Verona 13-15
tel: 0732 003 060; website: https://www.facebook.com/GradinaVerona/

HANUL BERARILOR CASA SOARE

The restaurant is spread across several rooms in this historic house. Good food in a lively atmosphere. Part of the City Grill group, there's another branch on Bd. Pache Protopopescu.
Str. Poenaru Bordea, nr. 2
tel: 021 336 8009, 0729 400 800; website: hanuberarilor.soare@citygrill.ro
Opening hours: Mon-Thur, Sun 08.00-00:00, Fri-Sat 08.00-02.00

HANUL LUI MANUC

An inn ever since its opening two centuries ago, Hanul lui Manuc is a huge restaurant set around a central courtyard. It is now managed by the City Grill group which serves excellent Romanian food.
Str. Franceză 62-64
tel: 0730 18.86.53; email: rezervari@hanumanuc.ro; website: www.hanumanuc.ro
Opening hours: Mon-Thurs, Sun 08.00-00.00, Fri-Sat 08.00-02.00

LA MAMA

With the slogan "like your mama at home", this is a low key and popular restaurant chain serving hearty Romanian dishes.
Barbu Vacarescu 3, Delea Veche 51; for full list of locations see http://www.lamama.ro/locatii/

LACRIMI SI SFINTI

Lively Romanian restaurant launched by poet Mircea Dinescu. Most of what's on offer - including the wine - comes from Dinescu's country estate.
Opening hours: Mon 18.30-01.00, Tues-Thurs 12.30 - 01.00, Fri-Sat 12.30 - 02.30, Sun 12.30-01.00.
Str. Sepcari 16
tel: 0725 558 286, 0372 773 999; email: contact@lacrimisisfinti.com; website: www.lacrimisisfinti.com

NUBA

Stylish Asian fusion and sushi restaurant, where a DJ takes over on Wednesday to Saturday nights.
Strada Grigore Gafencu 27
Opening hours: Monday 18.00-24.00, Tues-Sun 12.30-24.00
tel: 0768 22 68 22; website: www.nuba.ro

THE DIVAN

Excellent Turkish food, and well worth waiting for even though service can be a little slow at busy times. The outdoor terrace is very popular in summer.
Opening hours: 10.00-02.00
Calea Floreasca 111-113
tel: 021 539 1919; website: http://thedivan.ro

TRATTORIA IL CULCIO

Tasty Italian cuisine at several venues in Bucharest including their garden cafe next to the Romanian Atheneum (Str. Benjamin Franklin 1-3), and trattorias off Piata Amzei (Str. Mendeleev 14) and on Str. Calea Floreasca 118-120.
email: office@trattoriailcalcio.com; website: http://trattoriailcalcio.ro

VATRA

Authentic Romanian Food in quiet and cozy surroundings near Cismigu gardens, Vatra is deservedly popular.
Opening hours: 12.00-00.00
Str. Actor Ion Brezoianu 19
tel: 021 315 8375, 0721 200 800; email: vatra@vatra.ro; website: www.vatra.ro

NIGHTLIFE

18 LOUNGE
A little north of the city centre, 18 Lounge has a wonderful view over the green expanses of Herastrau Park.
Piata Presei Libere 3-5, City Gate South Tower, 18th floor
Opening hours: 12.00-23.30
tel: 0733 501 401; website: www.18lounge.ro

BICICLETA
Bicicleta has to win the prize for quirkiness among Bucharest's bars. If your drinking companion is less than scintillating, amuse yourself by trying to spot how many bicycle parts have been incorporated into the decor of this bar.
Opening hours: 4pm till late
tel: 0734 000 555; email: contact@bicicleta-bucuresti.ro; website: www.bicicleta-bucuresti.ro
Str. Lipscani 38

BRUNO WINE BAR AND BISTRO
This Parisian style wine bar has an exhaustive list of vino from Chile to the local Romanian reds and whites. The attic is wonderfully cosy in winter.
Opening hours: 16.00-00.00
Covaci Str. 3
tel: 021 317 1741, 0757 557 291; email: info@brunowine.ro; website: www.brunowine.ro

GRADINA EDEN
A bohemian hideaway in the centre of the city, behind the Stirbei Palace. Tables, cushions and hammocks are laid out under the trees - but in case this sounds a little too rural, there's also a good WiFi signal.
Opening hours: 16.00-02.00
Calea Victoriei 107
tel: 0744 510 687; website: https://www.facebook.com/pg/gradinaeden107/about/?ref=page_internal

INTERBELIC

Rated by many as having the best cocktails in town, Intervalic is also loved for its party atmosphere.
Opening hours: Sun-Thurs 17.00-02.00
Calea Victoriei 17
tel: 0723 693 526; website: https://www.facebook.com/pg/Interbelic-Cocktail-Bar

LABORATORUL DE COCKTAILURI

What could be better than a Cocktail lab? The decor reflects the name with bits of lab equipment that might make you feel like you're back in chemistry class at school and posters advertising prescription drugs.
Opening hours: 17.00-01.00
Srt. Stavropoleos 8, 1st floor
tel: 0737 356 746: email: laboratorcocktailuri@gmail.com; email: www.laboratordecocktailuri.ro

SKY BAR

This glamorous all-white bar serves food as well as cocktails and other drinks, all in front of arguably the best view of the city. The futuristic design includes water-filled walls and an artificial river.
Opening hours: 10.00- last person standing
Calea Dorobanti 155, 5th floor
tel: 0724 759 227; email: office@skybar.ro; website: www.skybar.ro

MEETING PEOPLE

The International Women's Association of Bucharest (www.iwabucharest.ro) has regular coffee mornings and a wide range of other activities. Membership is RON300 for the year. New members are entitled to attend the monthly newcomers' coffee for six months - a great way to meet fellow expats. The only downside is most of the events are during the day, which makes it difficult for working women to attend.

Couchsurfing.com has frequent meet ups for expats based in Romania as well as those just passing through the capital

Many of the events on Meetup.com are tech oriented, but if you got through the listings there is something for everyone - from book clubs to kraal maga, as well as several regular expat meet ups.

Internations.com has an active Bucharest chapter.

INSIDER Q&A WITH MATCHMAKER OANA TODORA OF UMBRELLA FOR TWO

Single Girl's Guide to Bucharest: Does dating in Romania differ from anywhere else in the world?

Oana Todora: Dating, even if casual, is taken seriously in Romania. Casual spontaneous conversation and small talk are not necessarily the strengths of our education. Maybe the perspective can and will change for the younger generation. Otherwise we tend to take things more seriously when it comes to dating and relationships. Men don't necessarily have a relaxed and playful approach. On a first date they tend to talk about general things, like their jobs, hobbies and routines.

SGG2B: Are Romanian men romantic?

OT: If by romantic you mean buying flowers, candies and candles in order to impress a woman, yes they are romantic and they pay a lot of attention to these things. They are generally open to being romantic although it's not in their blood to be spontaneous or creative in this area. They have good intentions and are open to suggestions. Romanian men are courteous and protective. They are educated to be careful and gallant to women in their manners; they open the door for the lady, pull out her seat or take her coat, maybe drive her home if it's late.

SGG2B: Are there any cultural issues foreign women should be aware of?

OT: Romanian man is still a traditional one. Most of them are guided by gender differences, thus the woman remains responsible for taking care of the house, family and children. Of course, that is not a rule and there are exceptions too. Some of them are more open and willing to get involved in helping her with the house, cleaning and maybe cooking for the family.

SGG2B: How can you tell if a man wants a serious relationship as opposed to a fling?

OT: If the man is really interested in a woman, he asks open questions, he wants to find out more about her, he calls her, he initiates communication. When a man likes a woman he takes the initiative. So if he wants you, it's not hard to see. He does not necessarily expect the first steps to be taken by the woman.

If the man wants just a one night stand, will put pressure on you, he will hurry things and he will push things to reach the physical level in a heartbeat.

However, if he wants a relationship, he will be patient, will invest time and will not rush things.

SGG2B: Are there any dating etiquette rules foreigner women should be aware of?

OT: Concerning the bill, the man in Romania has a traditional approach meaning he prefers to pay for the entire bill. The woman can offer to pay her part, but if he's firm in his decision to pay the entire bill (especially if he liked the date), she should leave it.

He is also aware of the practice of splitting the bill and he may take it into consideration as well.

If a woman asks a man out for a date, for sure he will not get upset and if he likes the girl, he will agree.

SGG2B: Has the way people date in Romania changed a lot over time?

OT: Today tools like Tinder or online dating are well known and used, especially for casual dating. Prior to a first date, people usually prefer to talk a few times and get to know each other better.

For one night stands he will prefer to arrange a quick date. For a relationship he will take into consideration more aspects, preferring to talk and get to know the person before.

SGG2B: Can you suggest some romantic venues for dates in Bucharest?

OT: There are some beautiful terraces in the north part of Bucharest, fancy restaurants in Herastrau Park or the old town, some discreet garden terraces. I can also suggest a visit to Mogosoaia Palace.

Umbrella for Two is the first matchmaking service in Romania dedicated to those searching for the right partner for a beautiful long-term relationship. We know that the interests and hobbies you have in common are very important for establishing a long-term relationship. Umbrella for Two brings together people with similar interests and life style, both professionally and personally.

Umbrella for Two's recipe is simple: we take the head hunting principles from professional recruiting, then we identify and attract the right person for you. We facilitate the connection between our members, and the rest goes on naturally. We are your partner in the search for that special someone. At Umbrella for Two the process is created so that it guarantees safety and comfort, and confidentiality is equally important to us as it is to you.

For more information, visit https://www.umbrellafortwo.ro

STYLE & SHOPPING

Shopaholics will be spoiled for choice in Bucharest. Not only are most of the European chains - Zara, Mango, H&M and so on - present at the growing number of modern malls in the city, there are also lots of quirky local designers, homegrown fashion chains and second hand shops.

Another piece of good news is that unlike many East European capitals, style in Bucharest is urban and funky rather than ultra glam - meaning you don't need to pack high heels. In fact you'll fit in better with the locals in flat boots in winter and flat pumps or sandals in summer.

You won't go wrong wearing black in Bucharest. A simple outfit with a bit of a quirky edge (a vintage accessory, interesting bag, etc) will take you to most places.

A warm coat is a must for a winter visit. There are usually one or two short sharp cold snaps when temperatures can plummet below -15C. Having said that, temperatures can quickly rally to well above zero, and you might need sunglasses a week later!

INSIDER Q&A WITH FASHION BLOGGER OLIVIA
IOANA DEJEU

*Single Girl's Guide to Bucharest: Is there a distinct
"Romanian style" or "Bucharest style", and if so, how
would you describe it?*

Olivia Ioana Dejeu: I think the Romanian style is a casual
one, that includes a lot of basics. Romanian designers also
have a thing for oversized cardigans, coats and sweaters.
During the day, the style is more relaxed, you will see a lot
of earthy tones. During the evening, you will see glam
outfits everywhere, high heels, clutches. Men usually like
to keep it cool, and have a very laid back attitude. I think
the Bucharest style is developing more and more, with
French influences.

SGG2B: How would you describe your personal style?

OID: I like to wear a lot of basics, jersey tops, simple comfy
cardigans, that are chic and elegant at the same time, in
the right combination. I think I would define it as simple,
with a touch of elegance and grace. I love prints and I like
black and white ensembles. They are so classic, and
elegant, and they can also save you from any situation.
Also, I'm into gold and silver accessories, that have a
simple design, and a bit of sparkle, small diamonds or semi
precious stones. My bag is always black and white. And I
have a lot of stuff to fit in it, since I am always on the run,
with my job, with blogging, having photoshoots, I always
need a make-up kit with me, combs, etc.

*SGG2B: What should a foreign tourist who wants to be
practical but also stylish pack for a visit to Bucharest?*

OID: Well, don't know if you have heard about this..but
Bucharest tends to be a city of extremes. If you're visiting
in summer, then pack just some light dresses, shorts and
crop tops, as it tends to get really hot. Must pack your

sunscreen and your favourite pair of sunglasses! If you're visiting in winter, then an oversized wool sweater, some jeans and boots would be fine. Oh and don't forget a fluffy scarf!

SGG2B: What are your top venues for a glamorous vacation in Bucharest?

OID: For the glitz and glam, you can dine in Herastrau Park, in the north of the city, where you have a lot of expensive restaurants, such as Nuba (great atmosphere), Biutiful (incredible design), Bonton (for the summer nights), Isoletta (food) or in one of the sky bars in the city (18 Lounge, Skybar Dorobanti, Sole).

Zexe is a very chic café is, you really have to be dressed up to have a coffee there! Might be a little snobbish, but hey, in Bucharest it isn't the only place where you can strut your Céline bag.

For sightseeing, you can take a walk on the large beautiful boulevards - Kiseleff boulevard, Calea Victoriei, Bvd Aviatorilor - have a croissant, and feel like you're in the centre of Paris. A must see are also the impressive Romanian Atheneum, and the Palace of Parliament, the second largest building in the world.

You can also see "the whole world" in half an hour. Near Piata Dorobanti, you can go through the streets of Athenes, Rome, Paris, Tokyo, Prague, The Hague. A definite must see! And a great opportunity to take amazing pics! If you are into seeing also the traditional side, you have to check out the Museum of the Romanian Peasant. You can also buy some unique handmade souvenirs or antiques there.

SGG2B: A big question for solo travellers is where they can feel comfortable dining alone. Would you recommend any cafes or restaurants for a woman travelling solo?

OID: For a single lady travelling alone, there are a few types of places you can go dine or wine alone. If you want to meet new people, expats, listen to good music, then a good option would be Control Club. It works as a pub and club, and chances are you're going to meet someone interesting there. Though the wine is not good there, if you're into the wine experience, you can have a great one at the Wine Bistrot. The Hilton cafe or the Double tree by Hilton can be good places for a young single lady to enjoy a glass of wine with or without company. Otherwise, if you want to have breakfast, I recommend Boutique du Pain. For the evenings, you can go pub crawling on your own, if you're feeling full of energy. In the old town centre, there are hundreds of pubs and cafes. Sitting at a bar, sipping a cocktail can be very relaxing, while watching passers by, as there are some places which offer a street view. The party season never stops here, it goes from Monday to Sunday, so be ready for a lot of new experiences!

SGG2B: Where are the best places to shop in Bucharest?

OID: In Bucharest, we have a bit of the Dubai culture of shopping malls. Meaning that they are everywhere. We don't have a lot of the Wien culture, going on a Saturday for a walk on the boulevard, and finding all the big shops.

We have all the big retailers, and some designers shops also (Band of creators, with Romanian designs), located in the centre.We have a lot of second hand stores, also, if you're looking for a bargain, located on bvd.Iuliu Maniu, or Rahova (but these aren't such nice neighbourhoods). You can find some good priced items all the way from Piata Universitatii to Piata Unirii, on the right side of the boulevard, in all those small shops, but you have to search a lot. We have a great outlet, Miniprix, and you can find a lot of high end brands at a bargain. I highly recommend this one!

The secret is to have a good look in these shops, and you will certainly find some mind blowing pieces!

Olivia Ioana Dejeu is a fashion blogger at Illustrious (https://illustriousbyolivia.wordpress.com/). She is also co-founder of fashion artisan concept store Wear& Tell in Zurich (https://www.facebook.com/wearandtell/).

WHERE TO SHOP

MALLS

MEGAL MALL
Bucharest's biggest and newest major mall. The only downside is that it's about a 600m walk from the nearest metro station, Piata Iancului.
Bulevardul Pierre de Coubertin 3-5
Opening hours: 10.00-10.00
www.megamallbucuresti.ro

PROMENADA
In the affluent north of Bucharest, Promenada has an excellent food court. Nearest metro: Aurel Vlaicu.
Calea Floreasca 246B
Opening hours: 10.00-10.00
www.promenada.ro

AFI PALACE COTROCENI
Deservedly Bucharest's most popular mall probably has the best selection of shops. It tends to be packed out on weekends so best times to visit are weekdays or early mornings.
Bulevardul Vasile Milea 4
Opening hours: 10.00-10.00
www.aficotroceni.ro

SUN PLAZA
Currently undergoing a renovation, the Sun Plaza has a good selection of shops and is accessible via an underpass directly from Piata Sudului metro station.
Calea Văcărești 391
Opening hours: 10.00-10.00
www.sun-plaza.ro

UNIREA SHOPPING CENTRE
Bucharest's most central shopping centre takes up a whole side of the huge Piata Unirii. It was originally opened in 1976 as Bucharest's central department store but converted into a mall in the 1990s. As well as brands like H&M, Koton and Stradvarius it also has a large selection of small private shops.
Piata Unirii
Opening hours: 10.00-10.00
www.unireashop.ro

BANEASA SHOPPING CITY
Romania's largest mall is next to Ikea on the road to the airport. Buses 131 and 301 travel between the mall and Piata Romana metro station.
Şoseaua Bucureşti-Ploieşti 42D
Opening hours: 10.00-10.00
www.baneasa.ro

LOCAL DESIGNERS

BAND OF CREATORS
Exclusive store close to the Athenaeum selling a long list of well known and brand new Romanian designers.
14, Benjamin Franklin

ATELIER AIUREA
Combines vintage fashions with quirky modern accessories, also offers styling services.
24 Gabroveni St., Bucharest
http://www.atelieraiurea.ro/

KINGA VARGA SHOWROOM
Local fashion designer takes traditional natural fabrics to high fashion.
Address: 10 Pictor Alexandro Romano St., Bucharest
http://www.kingavarga.ro

WM DESIGNER CONCEPT STORE
A "creative platform" of contemporary artists and designers.
63 Regina Elisabeta Blvd., Bucharest
http://www.wm-conceptstore.ro/

OANA MANOLESCU SHOWROOM
Local textile designer.
Address: 61 Dionisie Lupu St., Bucharest
http://www.oanamanolescu.ro/

CLOUD 9
Pop up store selling Romanian designers. See their Facebook page for details of events: https://www.facebook.com/cloud9magazine/

INTERNATIONAL DESIGNERS

Emporio Armani, Gucci and Max Mara all have outlets along the Calea Victoriei. Casa Frumoasa (Radisson Blu Hotel, Calea Victoriei 63-81) stocks a range of international designers.

LOCAL CHAINS

FORMAT LADY
100% made in Romania, Format Lady targets "active and elegant modern women" in the 30-50 age bracket.
Locations include: Piata Unirii 1, Bd. Magheru 18. http://www.formatlady.ro/index.php?controller=stores

LASHEZ
Street fashion brand Lashez has rapidly gained popularity and is expanding to Turkey and Moldova.
Locations include: Str. Lipscani 51, Promenada. http://www.lashez.com/shops/

NISSA

Nissa's very feminine collections aim to combine romance and classic chic.
Locations include: Bd. Dacia 39, Baneasa Shopping Centre.
http://www.nissa.com/mmxv/ro/magazine

MATHILDE

Quirky local brand.
Locations include: Bd. Nicolae Balcescu 22.
http://www.mathilde.ro/web/Top-Menu/Contact-magazine/index-en.html

SHOES

MUSETTE

High-end local vendor voted Romania's most fashionable brand.
http://musette.ro/ro/

Nexus. A nice selection of quality shoes and boots.
Calea Victoriei 134.

OUTLETS

MINIPRIX

A free for all of low priced high street seconds.
Bulevard Magheru 24A. Other locations at: https://www.miniprix.ro/magazine

ACCESSORIES

MELI MELO PARIS

AFI Cotroceni, Sun Plaza, Cora Pantelimon, Calea Mosilor 223 and others. https://melimeloparis.eu/pages/meli-melo-shops.html#bucharest

SPAS AND FITNESS

THERME
Therme Bucharest was an immediate success when it opened in January 2016. Billed as a "tropical paradise", the aqua park and spa centre is the largest in Europe with no less than eight heated pools. The centre is divided into three separate zones: the Palm is a relaxation zone, Elysium offers thermal saunas and massage, while Galaxy - the largest of the three zones - is a family area with wave pools and toboggan slides. Theme has been so successful, its owners are already planning to expand.

Located just outside Bucharest, a short drive from the airport, Therme operates its own buses from central Bucharest (see their website for routes and times).

Opening hours: Mon-Thurs 09.30-23.30, Fri 09.30-01.00, Sat-Sun 08.00-01.00
tel: 0311 088 888; email: contact@therme.ro; website: www.therme.ro
1 adult ticket RON39 for 3.5 hours, RON44 for 4.5 hours; RON54 day pass, concessions for children, students and families.

WORLD CLASS
The Romanian branch of the international fitness chain. Branches include at the Promenada and Mega Mall shopping centres and at the Hotel Radisson Blu on Calea Victoriei Nr. 63-81. They offer gym machines, aerobics and spinning classes and spa areas. See their website for contacts for each branch, schedules and prices. www.worldclass.ro

LADY FIT
Women only gym Lady Fit calls itself the "the first gym for delicate women"; in fact the Insanity, WonderWoman and BodyMakeOver classes are anything but delicate! Lady Fit has a full schedule of classes (see website), subscriptions range from RON35 for a single session to RON246 for unlimited access.

Str. Baratiei 35
tel: 0213 111 095, 0726 438 348; email: contact@ladyfit.ro;
website www.ladyfit.ro

KRAFT GYM
A small gym with workout machines and evening aerobics
classes.
Str. Anastasie Simu 7
tel: 0754 227 090; website: www.facebook.com/
kraftgym.ro/

BOOT CAMP
Erika runs intensive boot camps in Herestrau Park and
Pipera, see her Facebook page for details.
https://www.facebook.com/fittime.bucharest/

PURI BALI
A group of women from Bali have founded this massage
salon a stone's throw from the Atheneum. They give
excellent Balinese massage and a range of others including
reflexology and hot stone massages, as well as facials and
full spa rituals.
Str. Episcopiei 5, Parter, Apt. 2
tel: 0720.933.325; email: office@puribali.ro; website:
www.puribali.ro

ORHIDEEA HEALTH & SPA
The largest spa in Bucharest, Orhideea offers massage,
skincare rituals, a salt room and many other western and
eastern therapies. There is also a swimming pool and
hammam. Bookings must be made 24 hours in advance.
Calea Plevnei 145B
tel: 0215 696 360, 0742 099 094; email:
info@orhideeaspa.ro; website: www.orhideeaspa.ro

SANDAL SPA
A professional and welcoming spa in downtown Bucharest,
offering a full range of treatments, as well as hair and
makeup special occasions.

Bd. Unirii 18, building 5B, sc. 2, 4the floor, apartment 38 (intercom 038)
tel: 0761 733 737; email: office@sandalspa.ro; website: www.sandalspa.ro

GROOMING

It's not difficult to find a neighbourhood beauty salon, but a standards vary and we suggest asking an acquaintance for a recommendation or trying one of these:

LA BIBLIOTHEQUE
Combining beauty and books is a novel idea that works brilliantly. Browse, buy or simply borrow a book to read while you're having your beauty treatments.
Str. Duiliu Zamfirescu 10
tel: 021 212 5171; website: www.labibliotheque.ro

YVONNE SALON
Located on the ground floor of Promenada Mall, this chic salon is popular among expats living in north Bucharest as two of its stylists worked in London and speak fluent English.
tel: 021 312 6426; website: www.yvonnesalon.ro

SALON TRIBUTE
Friendly and professional salon off Calea Dorobanti.
Str. Londra 36
tel: 021.230.22.93, 0749.155.595; email: office@tributesalon.ro; website: www.tributesalon.ro

GETTING AROUND

Bucharest's metro, which opened in 1979, is the easiest way to get around town. The metro currently has four lines with a total length of 69.3 kilometres, and 51 stations. Several new lines are planned, including one to connect the city centre to the airport. Tickets cost RON5 for two, RON8 for a day pass and RON20 for a carnet of 10 tickets.

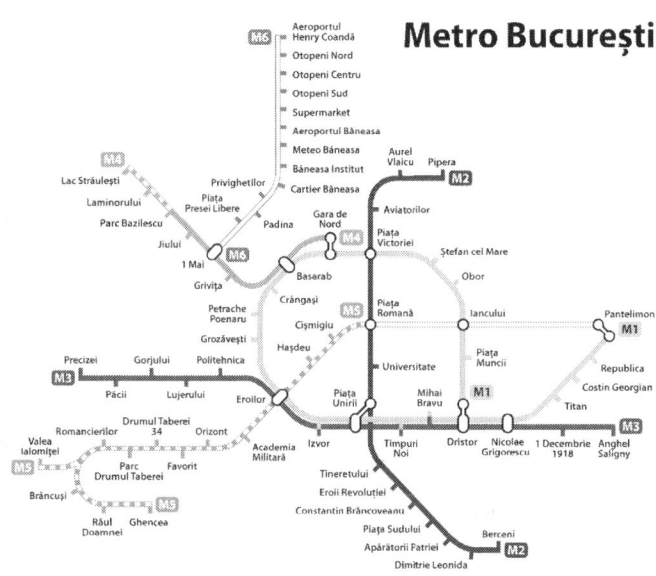

Solid lines show existing metro lines; dotted lines are under construction; while lines are planned.

Bucharest also has an extensive bus, tram and trolleybus network, useful for reaching parts of the city not served by the metro. Route maps are available at http://www.ratb.ro/eng/index.php

To use buses, trams or trolleybuses, you need to get a transport card from one of the kiosks next to most bus stops. A passport or other ID is required. Once you have your card, you can top it up as required for either single journeys or weekly or monthly passes. Don't forget to swipe it on one of the swipe pads when getting onto a bus as there are regular inspections.

The number of bicycle lanes in Bucharest are growing all the time. Electronic bicycle hire racks have opened in several locations including Universitate and Piata Revolutiei.

Car rental firms include sixt.com, avis.ro and eurocars.ro.

Yellow cabs operate in Bucharest and should use a meter (not all do). Check the price per kilometre on the side of the taxi before getting in - most will be in the RON1.39 - RON1.80 range; avoid any with higher prices. If the driver refuses to use the meter find another cab or fix a price before leaving. There are many reports of foreigners being overcharged by taxi drivers.

Taxi firms include Meridien, Cris Taxi, AS Taxi and many others. Some drivers will be reluctant to take passengers to the airport and at certain times of day it's difficult to find a cab in the city centre. Apps such as CleverTaxi and Star Taxi are widely used and easier than phoning for a cab.

Black Cabs is a somewhat expensive, but very reliable service, that has new clean cars with seatbelts, and English speaking drivers. Book online at Blackcabs.ro

Uber is increasingly popular in Romania, though there is some debate about whether it will continue to operate.

Romania's state railways operator CFR Calatori has a good online booking service, which is also 5% cheaper than buying tickets at the station. www.cfrcalatori.ro has an English language option for timetables and booking. When you buy your ticket, you will be sent a code by SMS, which you then enter into the site to download your ticket. Tickets can also be changed or cancelled (for a small fee) up to 24 hours before departure.

Soft Trans is a private rail operator that runs trains on a few routes. They are newer and cheaper than the CFR trains. Visit www.softrans.ro for information and booking.

Train is a quicker and better option than bus for both the Transylvanian cities and the Black Sea coast. www.autogari.ro has bus timetables and information on which of Bucharest's several bus stations to go to for each destination.

To visit Bran Castle and Peles Castle in a single day, take the Two Castles in One Day tour. Coaches leave from outside the Romanian Athenaeum at 8am, and the trip costs €75. Book online at www.bucharestcitytour.com.

DAY TRIPS

SNAGOV

Snagov is a popular lakeside resort 40 km north of Bucharest. It is set in Snagov Forest, the last remaining section of the huge Codrii Vlăsiei forest that once surrounded Bucharest and covered much of southern Romania. The trees started to be felled in the 19th century when the land was wanted for agriculture. The remains of Snagov Forest are now a protected area.

The village grew up around Snagov monastery, built in the 14th century on a small island in Lake Snagov. The monastery is believed to be where Vlad the Impaler, the inspiration for Bram Stoker's Dracula, was buried. The main mint of the medieval Wallachia principality was located on the island, and later an important printing press was set up there.

During communist times, the monastery was used as a retreat by Romanian leader Nicolae Ceaușescu. Former Hungarian Prime Minister Imry Nagy was briefly imprisoned there before being sent back to stand trial in Budapest.

After the collapse of communism, the Romanian government briefly considered building a Dracula theme park in Snagov, but the plans were dropped in 2006.

Some of the lakeside resorts include:

The swanky Snagov Club, which descries itself as a "relaxation oasis". The resort has pool bar with palm trees, a spa centre and three separate restaurants, as well as luxury hotel rooms.
Aleea Nufarului 1B

tel: +40 21 352 60 79, 0372 746 862 (club), 0736 862 119
(restaurant reservations);
email: reservation@snagovclub.ro; website:
www.snagovclub.ro

Dolce Vita is another luxury resort set on the shores of
Lake Snagov. It offers accommodation, a restaurant, a
children's playground and outdoor barbecue. There's
fishing and team sports for those looking to be more
active.
Parc Ponton 800
tel: 0723.580.780, 0786.251.029; email:
dolcevitasnagov@yahoo.com,
rezervaridolcevita@gmail.com; website:
www.dolcevitasnagov.ro

Numerous minibuses leave the public transport terminal
at Piata Presei Liberei in Bucharest for Snagov every day.
Take maxitaxi 443 to Siliştea Snagovului for the
monastery; it takes about one hour. The lake is about a
kilometre from the bus stop, and you can cross the bridge
or take a boat to the island. Check when the minibus will
return to Bucharest to avoid getting stranded in Snagov.

MOGOŞOAIA PALACE

Located just outside Bucharest on the shores of the
Mogoşoaia lake, Mogoşoaia Palace was built by the
Wallachian prince Constantin Brâncoveanu at the turn of
the 18th century. It was named after the widow of the
Romanian aristocrat, Mogoş, who owned the land where it
was built.

Brancoveanu didn't get to enjoy the palace for long. He
and his entire family were executed by the Ottomans in
1714, after which his palace was turned into an inn.
However, Prince Stefan Cantacuzino later purchased the
palace and returned it to Brâncoveanu's grandson
Constantin.

The building was virtually destroyed during the Russo-Turkish War of 1768-1774, but later rebuilt. In the 1920s and the 1930s, the palace once again became the centre of local and international high society and a location of political intriguing. Nationalised in 1945, the palace was turned into a museum 12 years later.

To reach the palace from Bucharest take bus 460 from outside the Parc Bazilescu metro station. Get off at the Mogoșoaia Palace stop.
Opening hours: Tues-Sun 10.00-18.00
tel: 021 350 6619

BRAN CASTLE

Towering dramatically over the Burzenland plain, Bran Fortress's stone turrets are as imposing now as they were centuries ago when this hilltop fortress repelled invaders from the south.

Teutonic knights originally built the wooden castle of Dietrichstein at the site in 1212, and it was replaced with a stone castle after being destroyed by Mongols invaders. It guards the old border between the mountains of Transylvania and Wallachia, the southern part of Romania that was under Ottoman rule until the mid 19th century.

Bran has been dubbed "Dracula's Castle", even though there is no evidence that the author Bram Stoker knew anything about Bran and its connections to Vlad the Impaler are tentative. In fact, Stoker was later found to have been thinking of a mountain far away in Moldavia when he envisaged Dracula's castle.

However, the castle was the favourite home of another famous Romanian, Queen Marie (1875-1938), and contains art and furniture collected by the queen. There is also a small open-air museum park displaying traditional Romanian peasant homes and barns from across Romania.

The debate over the ownership of Bran Castle erupted after the Romanian government passed a law allowing restitution claims on properties that were illegally expropriated by the communists in 2005. The following year, Bran was given back to Dominic von Habsburg, the son and heir of Princess Ileana, though this was later disputed by some MPs. More recently, there were reports that the castle had been put up for sale for €5mn.

Opening hours: April 1-September 1: Mon 12.00-18.00, Tues-Sun 09.00-18.00; October 1-March 31: Mon 12.00-16.00, Tues-Sun 09.00-16.00
Str. General Traian Mosoiu 24, Bran
tel: 0268 237 700, 0268 237-702; email: office@bran-castle.com; website: www.bran-castle.com

To reach Bran from Bucharest by public transport, take the train to Brasov then a bus from bus terminal No. 2. Buses go every 30 minutes on weekdays and hourly at weekends, and the journey takes about 45 minutes. It's also possible to take a taxi from Brasov for around €20. Bratax.ro run a professional taxi service with English speaking drivers - tel: 0268 315 555, 0726 315 555.

PELEȘ CASTLE

The favourite home of Romania's King Carol 1 and Queen Elisabeth (Regina Elisabetta), Peles Castle is a somewhat bizarre mix of the neo-renaissance and gothic revival styles set amid the towering peaks of the Carpathian Mountains.

Carol is believed to have built the palace, designed by German architect Johannes Schultz, after falling in love with the surrounding scenery - and it's easy to understand why.

The interior is just as lavish as the outside and almost oppressively ornate at times, with a mishmash of European styles from German to Italian. Schultz' original idea was apparently a huge version of an alpine villa.

Next to Peles Castle is the smaller Pelişor Castle, the home of King Ferdinand I and Queen Marie.

Sinaia is a 1.5 hour train journey from Bucharest, and it's possible to walk uphill to the castle, with much of the route up flights of steps set into the hillside. Otherwise, take a taxi from outside the station.

Opening hours: Mon-Sun 09.30-16.30
Aleea Pelesului 2, Sinaia
tel: 0244 310 918, 0244 312 184; email:
peles.ro@gmail.com, contact@peles.ro; website:
www.peles.ro

PROFILE: REGINA ELISABETTA

Carol I's wife, Elisabeth of Wied, was an unlikely match for the modernising king, being a dreamer, eccentric, prolific writer - and republican.

The German noblewoman married Prince Karl of Hohenzollern-Sigmaringen who had recently become Prince Carol of Romania, when he returned to Germany to find a wife.

The couple's early married life was marked by tragedy; their daughter Maria died at the age of three. Elisabeth never recovered from Maria's death.

However, she became an author of poems, plays, novels, short stories and essays under the pen name Carmen Sylva.

Carol's adopted heir Ferdinand later became the cause of a rift between the royal couple. Elisabeth encouraged Ferdinand's romance with one of her ladies in waiting, Elena Văcărescu, even though the heir to the throne was forbidden to marry a Romanian. When the affair was discovered both Elisabeth and Elena were exiled.

After her death, the queen became the cause of further controversy when it was discovered she had written in her diary that the republican form of government "is the only rational one".

WEEKEND TRIPS

BRAŞOV

Just two and a half hours by train from Bucharest, Brasov is dramatically different in culture and architecture. While Bucharest was under Ottoman rule for centuries, Brasov and the rest of the Transylvania region were part of the Hapsburg empire.

In the picturesque historic centre, tiny cobbled streets fan off from the central Str. Republic. Major sights include the gothic Biserica Neagră (Black Church), which dates back to 1477. The name was gained when the church was blackened by smoke from the great fire of 1689. It sits at the top of Str. Republic, on Piata Sfatului. The even older Biserica Sfante Nicolae is also well worth seeing.

Behind the Biserica Neagră are Braşov Citadel Fortress and Catherine's Gate, the only original city gate that has remained standing since medieval times. Nearby Strada Sforii (Rope Street) is one of the narrowest streets in Europe.

When it comes to eating, visitors are spoiled for choice along Str. Republic, where virtually every one of the pastel painted buildings is a cafe or restaurant, with shady tables set all along the middle of the street.

The city of just over 250,000 people is surrounded by the Southern Carpathians mountains, and a cable car transports passengers from the edge of the historic centre to the peak of nearby Mount Tampa - just a short walk from where the word BRASOV stands Hollywood-style on the side of the mountain. The views are spectacular.

LISTINGS

CASA WAGNER
Located on Brasov's main square in the heart of the city, this historic building offers modern comforts and many rooms have views of the Biserica Neagră and Mount Tampa.
5 Piata Sfatului
tel: 0268 411 253, 0727 800 367; website: www.casa-wagner.com

HOTEL BOUTIQUE CASA ANTIQUA
Another historic building in a great location, with cosy rooms and friendly staff.
Str. Republicii 22
tel: 0368 467 002, 0733 920 560, 722 208 529; em**ail**: contact@casaantiqua.ro; website: www.casaantiqua.ro

RESTAURANT BELVEDERE
Fine dining in a nicely decorated restaurant with good views.
Str. Stejarisului 11
tel: 0268 415 575, 0735 404 169; website: www.restaurantbelvedere.ro

DEI FRATI
Mediterranean food close to Piața Sfatului. Highly recommended.
Piata Enescu George 16
tel: 0724 216 028; website: https://www.facebook.com/Deifrati/

SIBIU

Formerly known as Hermannstadt, Sibiu's history within the Hapsburg empire is evident in the architecture along its cobbled streets. This area only became part of Romania after the First World War, and most of its population were ethnic Germans until 1941. Today their number has dwindled to a few thousand though they include Romania's most powerful man, President Klaus Iohannis, who served as mayor of the city for a decade.

For centuries, life in Sibiu has centred around the three squares that still form the heart of the historic city. The huge expanse of Grand Square is bordered by the Baroque Brukenthal Palace, the Jesuit Church and the large Art Nouveau building where the city hall is located. Overlooking the square is the Council Tower, a symbol of the city dating back to the 13th century (though it has been rebuilt several times). Passageways connect Grand Square to the smaller Lesser Square and Huet Square.

Also worth seeing are the History Museum, the Pharmacy Museum which is in one of the oldest apothecary shops in Europe, and the Traditional Folk Civilisation Museum.

Sibiu's rich cultural life was recognised when it was named the European Capital of Culture in 2007, an honour it shared with the city of Luxembourg. There are three theatres and a philharmonic orchestra based in the city, which also hosts numerous festivals. The most important is the Sibiu International Theatre Festival, held in Sibiu every spring, but there are also the Medieval, Artmania, Rockin' Transilvania, Jazz and several others.

Small wonder this beautiful city was ranked eighth on Forbes' 2008 list of the most idyllic places to live in Europe!
Just over 200 km from Bucharest, Sibiu is located in the Cibin Depression surrounded by three mountain ranges - the Făgăraş Mountains, the Cibin Mountains, and the Lotrului Mountains. It's around a five hour train journey from the capital, making it a comfortable weekend trip.

LISTINGS

PENSIUNEA CHIC
In a 14th century building in the heart of Medieval Huet Square, Pensiunea Chic has small but comfortable rooms.
Mos Ion Roata Nr.6

tel: 0759041405; email: booking@pensiunea-chic.ro;
website: www.pensiunea-chic.ro

DRAMA QUEEN INN
No drama here, just a warm welcome from its owner, and
excellent value for money close to the centre.
Tirgu Vinului 9
tel: 0747 514 296

MAX
Decent food in a pleasant atmosphere. Framed vintage
posters contrast with the rough, whitewashed walls of this
14th century residence, and there is an outside terrace.
Strada Ocnei 22
tel: 0269 233 003; email: info@max-restaurant.ro;
website: www.max-restaurant.ro

CRAMA ILEANA
Worth leaving the city centre for this traditional Romanian
restaurant with excellent service.
Piata Teatrului 2
tel: 0269 434 343; email: opreanmonica@yahoo.com;
website: www.cramaileana.ro

SIGHIŞOARA

Imagine yourself back in medieval times in this perfectly
formed jewel of a town set among the Transylvanian
mountains on the Târnava Mare river. The historic centre,
designated a UNESCO world heritage site, is easy to
explore, consisting of just a handful of streets around
central Piata Cetatii, all lined with houses painted in
glowing colours.

Sighişoara, like Sibiu and Brasov, is one of the
Siebenbürgen founded by the Transylvanian Saxons.
Formerly known as Schassburg, it was built on the site of
the Roman Castrum Stenarum settlement by the German
craftsmen and merchants who moved there in the 12th

century, though most of the historic centre dates from the 16th century. The small city was fortified strongly to repel Turkish raiders as the Ottoman empire advanced on Central Europe.

Nine medieval towers built by craftsmen's guilds are still standing. The Clock Tower, or Council Tower, which dates from the 14th century, is the city's top attraction. At the top of the tower is the two-plate clock, set with carved figurines representing Peace, Justice, Law and the pagan gods for whom the days of the week are named. The views of Sighișoara's cobbled streets and the surrounding countryside from the top of the tower are spectacular.

Other towers include the Blacksmiths' Tower (Turnul Fierarilor), Butchers' Tower (Turnul Macelarilor), Cobblers' Tower (Turnul Cizmarilor) and Tailors' Tower (Turnul Croitorilor).

Near the Clock Tower on Piata Cetatii - once the site of markets, public executions and witch trials - is the Church of the Dominican Monastery, while the Scholars' Stairs lead from the square up to the gothic Church on the Hill.

Sighisoara's other claim to fame is as the birthplace of Vlad Tepes, also known as Vlad the Impaler or Dracula, who was born in the town after his father Vlad Dracul was sent there in exile. The ground floor of his surprisingly pretty ochre painted house at Str. Cositorarilor 5 is now a restaurant, while the museum of weapons is on the first floor. If this whets your appetite for the gruesome side of medieval life, the Torture Room (Camera de Tortura) is at the base of the Clock Tower. Tickets for the History Museum give entry to all three.

Clock Tower (Turnul cu Ceas)
Piata Cetatii
Opening hours: May 15 - September 15: Tues-Fri 09.00-18.30, Sat-Sun 10.00-17:30
September 16 - May 14: Tues-Fri 09.00-15:30, Sat-Sun 10.00-15:30

History Museum (Muzeul de Istorie)
Piata Muzeului 1, inside the Clock Tower; opening hours
same as for Clock Tower.
tel: 0265 771.108

The Church on the Hill (Biserica din Deal)
Piata Cetatii
Opening hours: Mon-Sun 10.00-18.00

LISTINGS

HOTEL VILLA FRANCA
Str. 1 Decembrie 1
tel: 40 758 837 792; email: vilafranka@gmail.com;
website: www.vilafranka.ro/contact.php
Cheap, central and decorated in a quirky mix of modern
and traditional.

CASA GEORGIUS KRAUSS
Str. Bastionului 11
tel: 0365 730 840; email: contact@casakrauss.com;
website: www.casakrauss.com
Located in a Unesco certified building dating back to 1600,
Casa Georgius Krauss is in the medieval citadel just two
minutes from the central square. It is the former home of
historian Georg Krauss. Great service and an excellent
restaurant.

CAFFE MARTINI HABERMANN
Piata Hermann Oberth 42
tel: 0751 169 309; website: www.facebook.com/
cafemartinin?rf=159101327548012
Good food and service, popular with both locals and
tourists.

RESTAURANT CASA VLAD DRACUL
Str. Cositorarilor 5
tel: 0265 771 596; website: www.casavladdracul.ro
Dine on traditional Romanian food in the medieval setting
of Dracula's former home.

Three direct trains run from Bucharest to Sighisoara daily, taking a little over five hours. There are more services via Brasov.

Bus companies FANY and Memento Bus run daily services from Bucharest to Sighisoara, leaving from Autogara Filaret and Autogara CHR respectively.

CONSTANȚA AND THE BLACK SEA COAST

Just a two hour train ride from Bucharest, Constanta is both a jumping off point for the Black Sea coast and a fascinating historic city in its own right.

Constanța is Romania's fifth largest urban area and the oldest continuously inhabited city in the country, with a rich history form the Roman era and before. Its original name, Tomis, came from its legendary foundation by Tomyris, queen of the Massagetae group of nomadic tribes. Jason is said to have landed in Tomis with the Argonauts after finding the Golden Fleece.

One of its most renowned residents was the Roman poet Ovid, who was exiled here by Emperor Augustus in 8AD. He was unimpressed by the town where he spend the last eight years of his life, describing its location in a "war-stricken cultural wasteland".

There's a lot of visible reminders of Constanta's Roman past in the present day city. The Roman Mosaic Edifice was discovered in 1959 under the central Ovidiu Square. The building - once the largest of its kind in the Roman empire - linked the port and the ancient city.

The pedestrianised old town around Ovidiu Square is popular with locals and tourist alike; restaurants have tables outside for most of the year. The old Casino is a stunning art nouveau building right out on the sea near the port - one of the largest in Europe. The seaside boulevard near the casino is also a popular place for a stroll, especially at sunset. Also worth a look are the St. Peter & Paul Orthodox Cathedral and the Great Mahmudiye Mosque - witness to the city's time under both Christian and Muslim leaders.

Immediately northeast of Constanta city centre is Romania's most popular tourist resort, Mamaia. Hotels and restaurants have been built all along the 8km long strip of land between the Black Sea and Lake Siutghiol. A cable car transports people along the spit, with great views over the sea. Mamaia throngs with holidaymakers in the summer, but becomes a ghost town in winter. Avoid the beaches at the far end of the spit closest to Constanta, where waste is channeled into the sea.

LISTINGS

BELLE EPOQUE BOUTIQUE VILLA
Pricey but worth it, the Belle Epoque Boutique Villa is located in a historic building just 200m from central Ovidiu Square. The rooftop terrace has panoramic views of the port.
Str. Sulmona nr. 28
tel: 0770 587 357; website: https://www.facebook.com/BelleEpoqueVilla/

HOTEL CAROL
Another converted historic building, Hotel Carol is close to the sea front and Art Museum. The rooms are decorated with classic silk wallpaper and Victorian furniture, but it also has a small but modern fitness centre.
Str. Mihail Kogalniceanu nr. 15
tel: 0241 552 100; email: hotelcarol@gmail.com; website: www.carolhotel.ro

TOMIS GARDEN APARTHOTEL
Located on the lagoon side of the spit, this aparthotel is less than 200m from the beach and has attractive modern studios with balconies. Self-catering facilities are a bonus as with most restaurants in Mamaia you're paying for location - not quality of food!

Bulevard Mamaia 430A
tel: 0241 480 975, 0737 144 804; email:
contact@tomisgarden.ro; website: www.tomisgarden.ro

BYBLOS LEBANESE RESTAURANT
Excellent food in this popular, eclectically decorated
restaurant.
Bulevard Tomis 48
tel: 0732 818 845; email: restaurant@byblos-constanta.ro;
website: www.byblos-constanta.ro

CAFE DEL MAR MAMAIA
Good Mediterranean food and pleasant service.
Bulevardul Mamaia
tel: 0744 681 681; email: office@cafedelmarmamaia.ro;
website: www.cafedelmarmamaia.ro

PREDEAL

At over 1,000 metres above sea level, Predeal is Romania's
highest town and its top ski resort. It's the perfect place to
escape the heat of Bucharest in summer - temperatures are
usually around 10C below those in the capital.

The small mountain town is spread out along the main
Bucharest-Brasov highway and across the Prahova valley.
Guesthouses and luxury villas jostle for space in the
narrow valley, but there are also a fair large number of
abandoned older buildings in the town, a legacy of
Romania's dwindling population.

A short walk along the N1 highway from the town centre is
the Nativity of the Virgin Mary monastery, one of the
oldest churches in the region. While the current building is
around 200 years ago, it was built on the site of a
hermitage built in 1744. Predeal's first school was founded
in one of the monastery's cells. The monastery was shut
down in the communist era but the buildings were left
standing and it was reopened as a convent in 1993.

Snowfalls are expected in Predeal between September and March, and there are five major ski runs around the town, ranging in length from 790 metres to 2,243 metres. Predial is also popular for trekking, and there are some good hikes from the top of the ski lifts.

Trains from Bucharest's Gara de Nord take around two hours, depending on whether it's a fast or slow train. Memento bus operates a service from Autogara CHR taking just over three hours.

LISTINGS

CASA DEL SOL
Family run guest house with stunning views over the Prahova Valley. Breakfast is excellent.
Str. Ceahlău 12,
tel: 0747 318 475; email: rezervari@casadelsolpredeal.ro, office@casadelsolpredeal.ro; website: www.casadelsolpredeal.ro

PREDEAL COMFORT SUITES
Popular among skiers, Predial Comfort Suites offers a sauna, fitness centre, indoor swimming pool and spa. There's also a bar and Lebanese restaurant on site. All the rooms have a four-poster beds.
Strada Trei Brazi
tel: 0744 587 838; email: marketing@comfort-suites.ro; website: www.predealcomfortsuites.ro, www.facebook.com/predealcomfortsuites/

DRAGULUI
Easy to spot in summer because of its terrace bordered by colourful window boxes, Dragului is deservedly Predial's most popular restaurant. Service is generally good, though there can be a wait of 30 minutes during busy times.
Bulevardul Mihai Saulescu 28
tel: 026 845 5482; email: hotel_dragului@yahoo.com; website: www.restaurantdragului.ro

RESTAURANT HANUL DOMNITORILOR

Serves traditional Romanian food; generous portions and good service.
Bulevardul Mihail Saulescu 32-34
tel: 0766 531172; website: www.facebook.com/pages/
Hanul-Domnitorilor-Predeal/186835668045185

RESTAURANT MIORITA

Attractive restaurant with good food in a friendly ambiance.
Strada Trei Brazi 6
tel: 026 845 5150

COMMUNICATIONS

POST

Romania's state postal service is Posta Romana. Find a nearby post office at: https://www.posta-romana.ro/en/find-a-post-office.html

Posta Romana's record in delivering letters and parcels from abroad is patchy. Sending from the UK, the safer (though pricier) option is to send mail using international tracked postage. Mail sent using this service will be delivered to addresses in Romania by private courier service GLA. Use the track and trace service on their website to track your parcel's progress: https://gls-group.eu/RO/en/home

MOBILE TELECOMS

The main mobile providers in Romania are Orange, Vodafone and Telekom, providing both contracts and pay as you go cards. Roaming prices in Romania are comparable to other EU countries.

WiFi

Most cafes and bars in Bucharest provide free wifi. You may need to ask for the password ("parola" in Romanian). There's also WiFi in some taxis, supermarkets, shopping malls, and many other places - even the forest-like Kiseleff Park has a good signal.

INTERNET CAFES

Given the spread of both Wifi and mobile internet, the number of internet cafes has dwindled. Some options are:
Maxinet Internet Cafe, Str. Academiei 9
One Tech Cafe, Parter bloc, Str. Ion Câmpineanu 22
Kitty Cafe, Str. Știrbei Voda
Discovery Arena - Internet Cafe, Strada Elena Cuza 42

SAFETY

CRIME

Crime rates in Bucharest are relatively low compared to most major European capitals. Central Bucharest is particularly safe, with a heavy security presence; there are security guards outside many businesses, clubs and restaurants, in parks and other areas.

Cristian Ciobanu published the Bucharest Fear Map in 2012 as part of his PhD research. The fascinating map is based on the perceptions of Bucharest residents of districts of the city. Respondents were asked to rate each neighbourhood on a range of one to five from "very safe" to "dangerous".

The safest rated districts were almost all in the northern part of the city, with Primăverii, Aviației and Herăstrău among the best ranked, along with the tony Cotroceni district.

At the other end of the scale, respondents agreed almost unanimously that the southern Rahova - Ferentari district was by far the most dangerous area. Ferentari is considered a no go area by most Bucharest residents and you are unlikely to have any reason to visit. Warning signs were also raised about Ghencea in the north, the Colentina - Baicului - Pantelimon area in the northeast and Giulesti in the northwest. It should be noted that the survey is based on perceptions, not actual crime figures.

The same precautions to avoid petty crime should be taken as in any large city. Pickpocketing and bag snatching are common on public transport, in and around stations, outside the airport, and in crowded areas throughout the city. Be especially cautious around bureaux de change.

According to the British foreign office, there have been cases of organised attacks by groups, often including children. Usually some members of the group create a distraction, while others try to snatch watches and jewellery from their target. Another warning concerns thieves who pretend to be plain-clothes policemen and demand to inspect passports and wallets.

If you are staying in a hotel, use the safe to store documents and avoid carrying valuables with you or leaving them in the room. Carry a photocopy of your passport in case you are required to show your ID.

We recommend that you don't risk breaking the law. Drug-related offences can carry a prison sentence. It is illegal to drink and drive. It is also illegal to change money on the streets, and photography is forbidden in sensitive areas including most airports and military bases and the Bucharest metro.

HEALTHCARE AND INSURANCE

Make sure you have travel insurance, and if you're from an EU country, you can obtain a free European Health Insurance Card (EHIC) that entitles you to emergency care in Romania.

EARTHQUAKES

Southern and southwestern Romania including the Bucharest area are in an earthquake zone. The most serious recent earthquake was in 1977 when 1,578 people, including 1,424 in Bucharest, were killed and over 32,000 buildings were damaged or destroyed.

There are frequent small tremors in Bucharest that do not cause any damage, but it's worth being prepared for a more serious quake.

A US government campaign to promote earthquake preparedness recommends:
* Locate a safe place to shelter in case of an earthquake, for example under a sturdy piece of furniture or against an interior wall, and away from windows or items that can fall on you.
* Make sure you know where your important documents (passports, money) are, and have a supply of water and food.
* During the earthquake: stay where you are until the shaking stops (do not go outside).
* Drop, Cover, and Hold On - Drop to the ground, Cover your head and neck with your arms, and if a safer place is nearby, crawl to it and Hold On.
* If you are outside, move away from buildings, streetlights or anything that can fall on you. In a city, you may need to go inside a building to avoid falling debris.

BOOKS

GUIDEBOOKS

Lonely Planet Romania & Bulgaria (2013) The ubiquitous Lonely Planet's guide to Romania and neighbouring Bulgaria has a substantial chapter on Bucharest, with insider tips and pithy reviews.
The Rough Guide to Romania (2016) Newly updated, the Rough Guide is strong on culture and historical context, and very readable.
The Rough Guide Snapshot Romania: Bucharest (2016) A cheap kindle-only version of the Bucharest chapter from the Rough Guide to Romania.
Bucharest Tourist Guide: Pocket Edition (2015) Bilingual English-Romanian guide giving a rundown of the main attractions.
City Compass Romania: Bucharest & Beyond (2016) Guide targeting expats in Bucharest, with personal insights from locals and foreigners plus the useful business directory.

FICTION

Manning, Olivia. The Balkan Trilogy
The first two volumes of Olivia Manning's stunning semi-autobiographical trilogy are set in Bucharest at the beginning of the Second World War. Manning paints a vivid portrait of the almost feudal Romanian society and its many intrigues between rival factions, as well as the intimate account of her young British protagonists, Harriet and Guy Pringle.
Radulescu, Romnica. Black Sea Twilight
Written from the perspective of a tempestuous young artist, Black Sea Twilight is ultimately a love story between Romanian Nora and her ethnic Turk childhood friend Gigi. Set in the seaside town of Mangalia in the late communist years, it sensitively handles the issues of illegal abortion and drug addition.
Ormsby, Mike. Never Mind the Balkans, Here's Romania

This collection of short stories paints an incisive yet sympathetic picture of Romania and Romanians that earned Ormsby the title "our British Caragiale" - after Romania's famous Victorian era satirist.

Grigoras, Emanuel. The Right Place

Grigoras tells the story of a group of young, single people working in Bucharest in the last years of communism. Unfortunately, his clever storytelling is let down by the poor translation into English.

NON FICTION

Kaplan, Robert D. In Europe's Shadow: Two Cold Wars and a Thirty-Year Journey Through Romania and Beyond

Kaplan's book is the culmination of visits to Romania from the 1970s to the 2010s, during which time it transformed from a bleak Communist backwater to a modern European nation. He brings together memoir, travelogue, journalism and history in a book that goes beyond Romania to shed light on some of the broader questions of our times.

Behr, Edward. Kiss the Hand You Cannot Bite: Rise and Fall of the Ceausescus

A vividly written account of the lives of Romania's Communist dictator Niculae Ceausescu and his wife Elena. Behr outlines how the Ceausescus were able to take and hold onto power until their dramatic fall in 1989.

TRAVEL WRITING

Fermor, Patrick Leigh. Between the Woods and the Water: On Foot to Constantinople from the Hook of Holland: The Middle Danube to the Iron Gates

Patrick Leigh Fermor set off across Europe from Holland to Turkey in the 1930s, when he was just 18. This beautifully written book is the second part of his memoir, taking him from the Danube down through Hungary and Romania.

Eames, Andrew. Blue River, Black Sea

Eames' journey along the Danube is a homage to Fermor, but his quirky writing and entertaining accounts of the modern-day characters he meets along the way makes it all his own.

Dunlop, Tessa. To Romania With Love

18-year-old Tessa Dunlop went to Romania to work in an orphanage. What followed was a love affair with Romania and Romanians. Dunlop, now a BBC presenter, gives a painfully honest account of her experience at the orphanage, and later her relationship with Vlad, the young son of her host family.

LANGUAGE

The Romanian language is a Romance language, from the same family as languages such as French, Spanish and Italian, meaning if you speak one of these language you will have an advantage in learning Romanian.

Romanian is the native language of around 24 million people, mainly in Romania and neighbouring Moldova, where it has official status.

It is part of the Balkan-Romance group, also known as the Vlach languages, which evolved from Vulgar Latin in Southeast Europe after separating from the Western Romance group starting from the 5th century. Romanian therefore includes numerous words from the Slavic languages spoken in most of the region, as well as from French, German, Greek and Turkish.

While Romanian is the only Vlach language widely spoken, there are also a small number of Vlach speakers in Serbia and speakers of the South-Danubian languages in Greece and Macedonia.

LANGUAGE COURSES

Bucharest has two excellent language schools that provide Romanian courses for foreigners.

Rolang School offers beginner, intermediate and advanced courses for adults. There's an eight week course with lessons two evenings a week and a two week intensive programme, as well as specialist courses such as Romanian for business and cultural integration. The cost for most modules is €230.
www.rolang.ro email: office@rolang.ro tel: 0734 936 290
Calea Tudor Arghezi 28

Romanian Cultural Institute has a similar set of eight-week and intensive courses at €200 or RON800 per module, plus its "Let's sit over a glass of wine!" conversation and "Grammar tips" workshops at RON400.
www.icr.ro email: icr@icr.ro tel: 031 710 0627, 031 710 0606
Aleea Alexandru 38

Casa Paleologu runs a one-day workshop on the Romanian mentality for foreigners each year, usually in March.
www.paleologu.com email: cursuri@paleologu.com tel: 072 227 7764
Calea Armenească 34

BASIC ROMANIAN

GREETINGS
Hi - Buna (boo-ner)
Good morning - Bună dimineața - (boo-ner dee-mee-na-tzah)
Good day (use during the afternoon) - Bună ziua (boo-ner zee-wah)
Good evening - Bună seara (boo-ner syah-ra)
Good night - Noapte bună (nwap-tay boo-ner)
Good-bye - La revedere (lah reh-veh-dah-reh)
Bye - Pa (pah)
See you soon - Pe curând (pay cur-oond)
How are you? - Ce mai faci? (chay my fach)
Fine, thank you - Bine, mulțumesc (bee-nay mul-t-mesk)

BASICS
Yes - Da (dah)
No - Nu (noo)
Please - Vă rog (vah rog)
Thank you - Mulțumesc (mul-t-mesk) or merci (mer-ci)
You're welcome - Cu plăcere (koo plah-chair-reh)
Excuse me - Pardon (par-don)
I'm sorry - Îmi pare rău (oohm pah-reh rauw)

LANGUAGE
I don't speak Romanian - Nu vorbesc românește (noo vor-besc roh-moohn-esh-tay)
Do you speak English? - Vorbiți engleză? (vor-bitz eng-lay-zeh)
I don't understand - Nu înțeleg (noo een-teh-leg)

EATING OUT
The menu, please - meniu, vă rog (menu, vah rog)
I would like... - Aș dori (ash do-ri)
The bill, please - Nota de plată, vă rog (no-tah deh plah-ta, vah rog)

AROUND TOWN
Where is the...? - Unde este...? (oon-day yest)
station - gara (gah-rah)
museum - muse (moo-zay-ooh)
cathedral - catedrală (cat-eh-draa-lah)
supermarket - supermarket (see-per-mar-ket)
tourist office - biroul turistic (bir-ool tut-is-tick)
toilet - toaletă (to-wha-lay-tah)

left - stânga (stan-geh)
right - dreapta (dray-yap-ter)
straight ahead - drept inainte (drept un-ain-tah)

GETTING TO KNOW PEOPLE
What is your name? - Cum vă numiţi? (coom vah n'-mits)
My name is... - Numele meu e... (noo-me-le men-oo yeh)
Nice to meet you - Încântat (un-koon-tat)
Where are you from? - De unde sunteţi? (day unday sin-tetz)
I am from... - Sunt din (sunt din)
England - Anglia (an-glee-yah)
USA - Statie (sta-tee-yay)
France - Franţa (fran-tza)
Germany - Germania (ger-man-ee-yah)
China - China (chee-nah)
Are you free tonight? - Sunteţi liber deseara? (sin—tetz leeber de-syah-rah)
Are you married? - Sunteţi căsătorit (m) / căsătorita (f)? (sin-tetz ca-sa-toh-ree-tah)
I am married - Sunt căsătorit (m) / căsătorita (f) (sunt ca-sa-toh-ree-tah)
I am single - Sunt singur (sunt seen-gor)
I Love you - Te iubesc (tay yoo-besk)

NUMBERS
1 unu (oo-noo)	6 sase (shasay)
2 doi (doy)	7 sapte (shaptay)
3 trei (tray)	8 opt (opt)
4 patru (patroo)	9 noua (noo-ah)
5 cinci (chinch)	10 zece (zechay)

MAPS

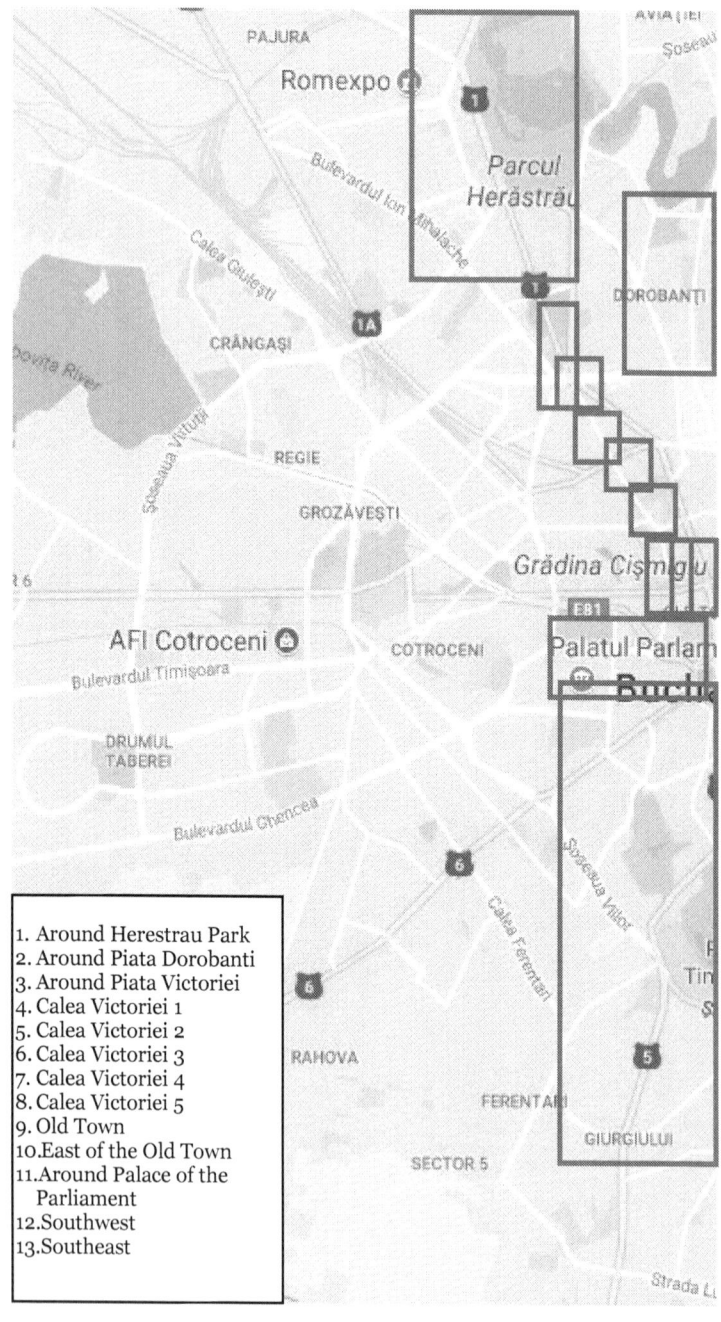

THE SINGLE GIRL'S GUIDE TO BUCHAREST

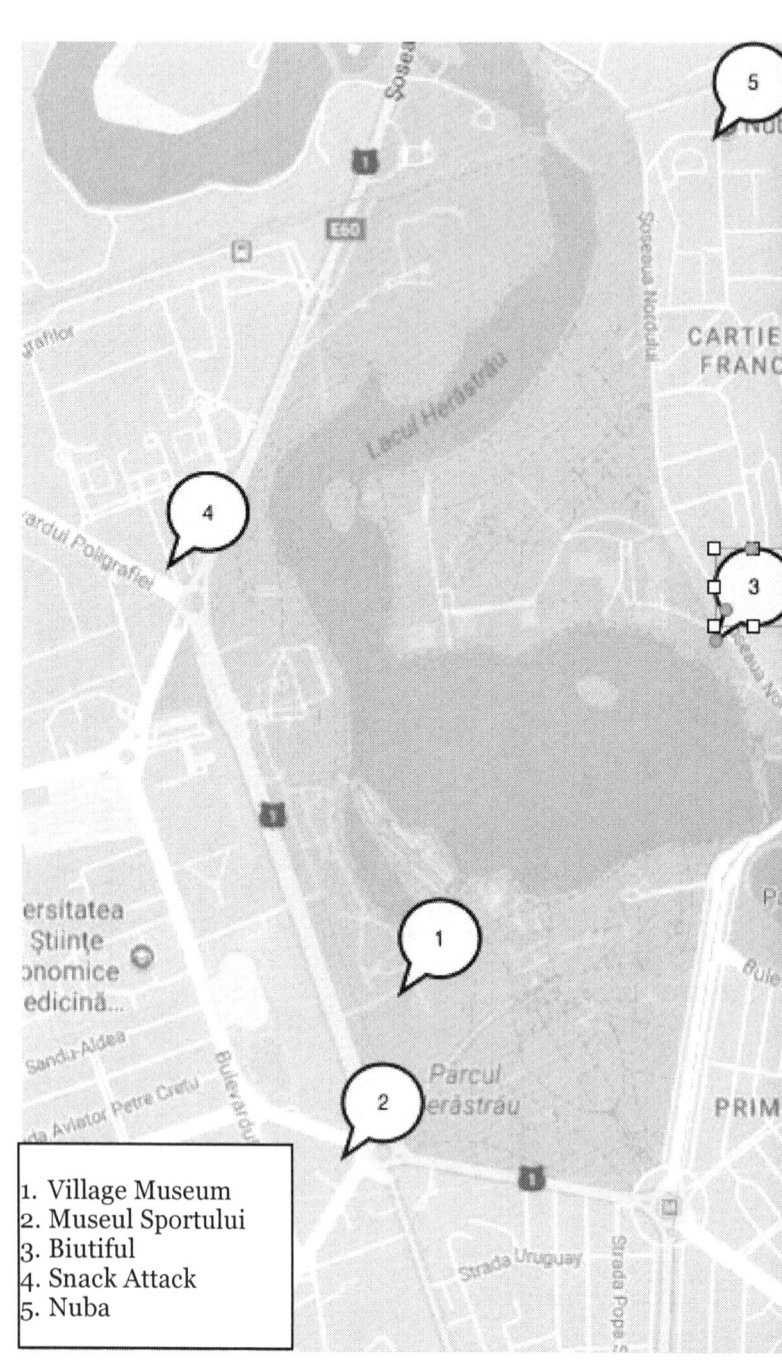

1. Village Museum
2. Museul Sportului
3. Biutiful
4. Snack Attack
5. Nuba

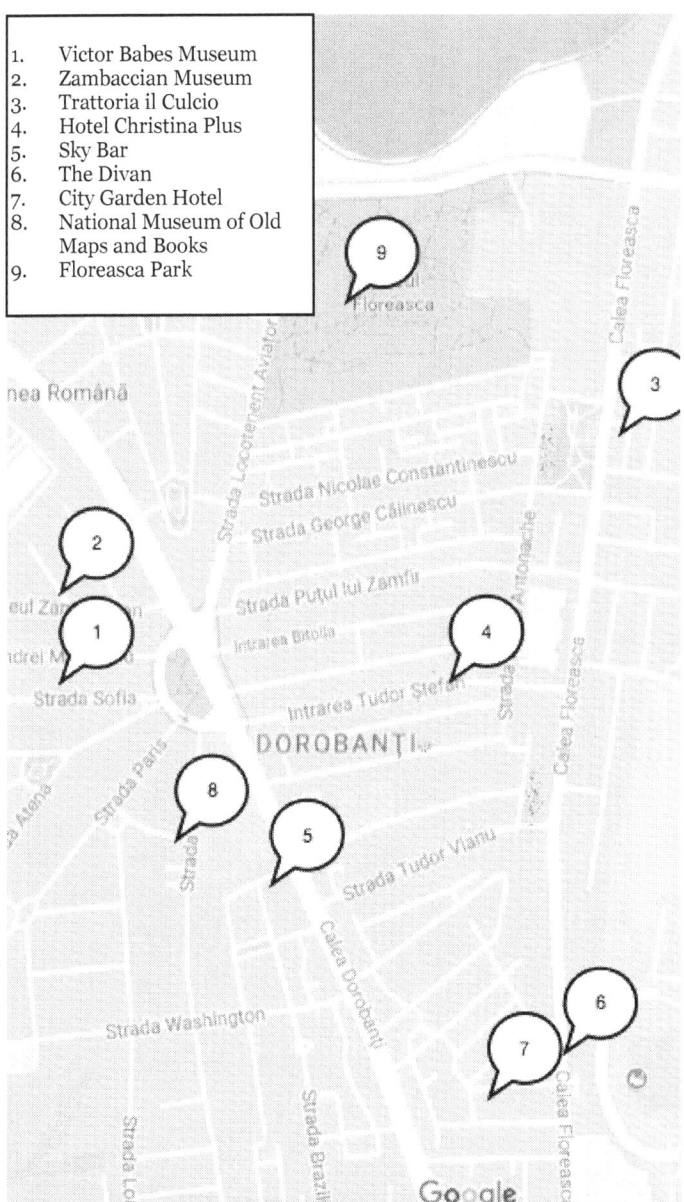

1. Victor Babes Museum
2. Zambaccian Museum
3. Trattoria il Culcio
4. Hotel Christina Plus
5. Sky Bar
6. The Divan
7. City Garden Hotel
8. National Museum of Old Maps and Books
9. Floreasca Park

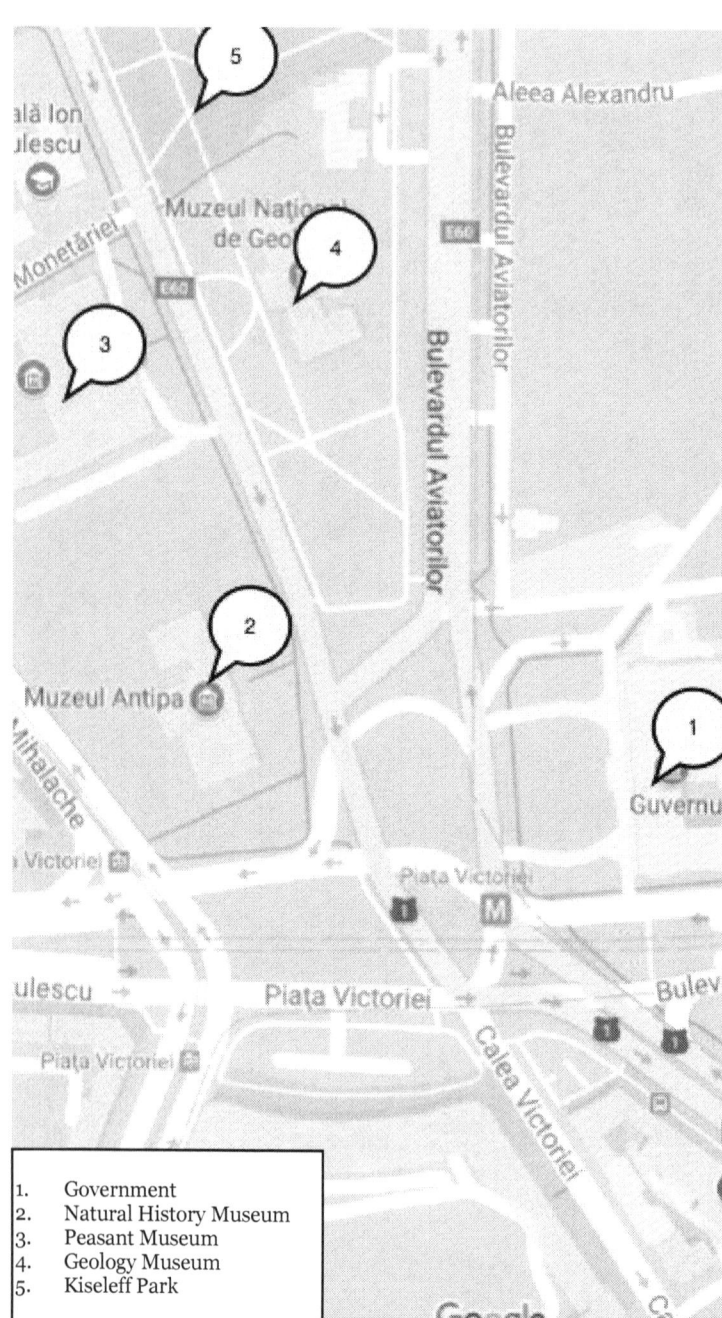

1. Government
2. Natural History Museum
3. Peasant Museum
4. Geology Museum
5. Kiseleff Park

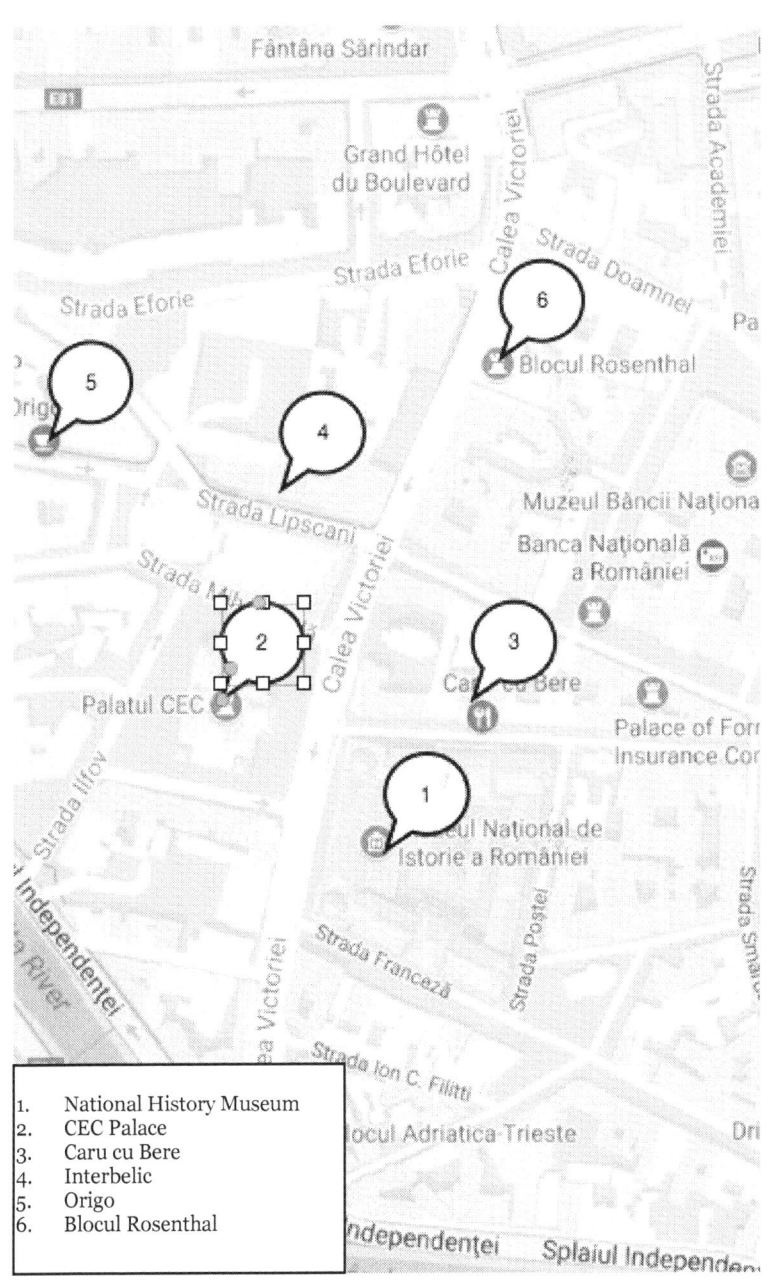

1. National History Museum
2. CEC Palace
3. Caru cu Bere
4. Interbelic
5. Origo
6. Blocul Rosenthal

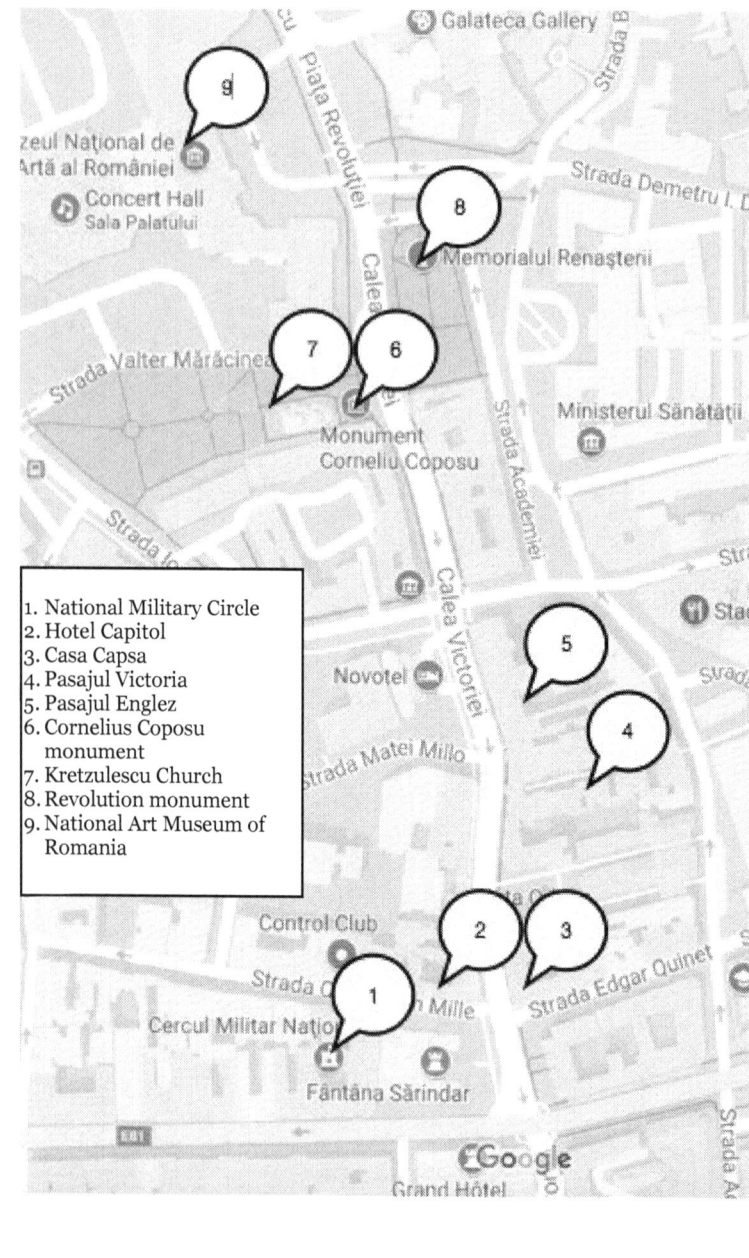

1. National Military Circle
2. Hotel Capitol
3. Casa Capsa
4. Pasajul Victoria
5. Pasajul Englez
6. Cornelius Coposu
   monument
7. Kretzulescu Church
8. Revolution monument
9. National Art Museum of
   Romania

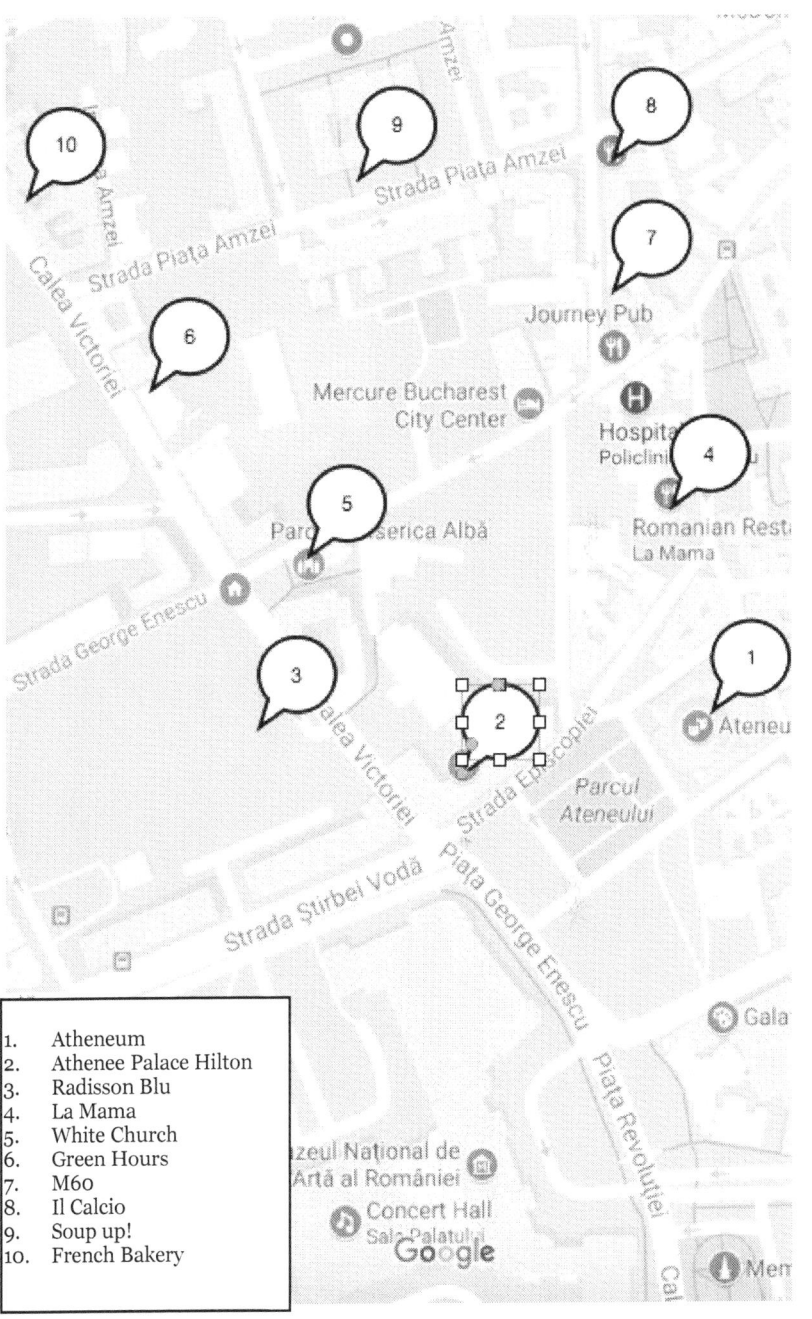

1. Atheneum
2. Athenee Palace Hilton
3. Radisson Blu
4. La Mama
5. White Church
6. Green Hours
7. M6o
8. Il Calcio
9. Soup up!
10. French Bakery

THE SINGLE GIRL'S GUIDE TO BUCHAREST

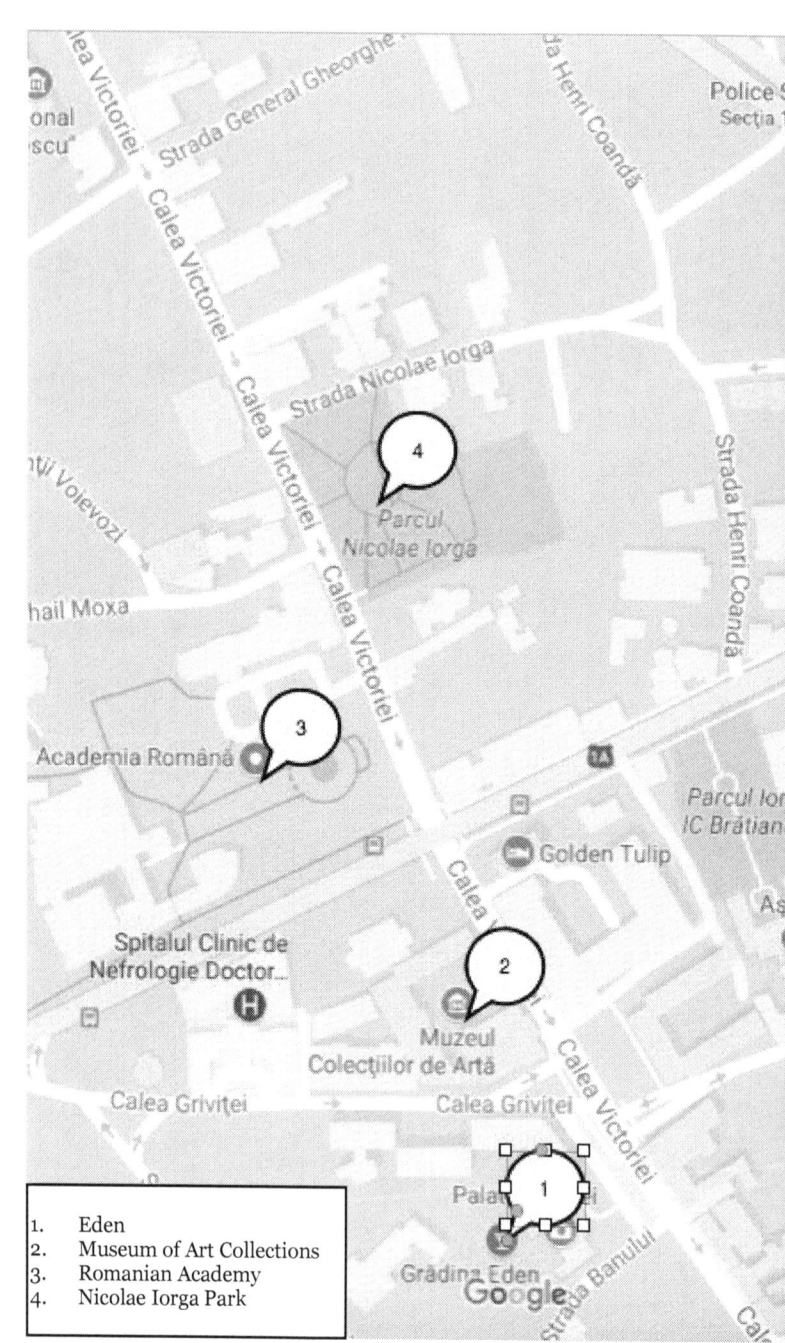

1. Eden
2. Museum of Art Collections
3. Romanian Academy
4. Nicolae Iorga Park

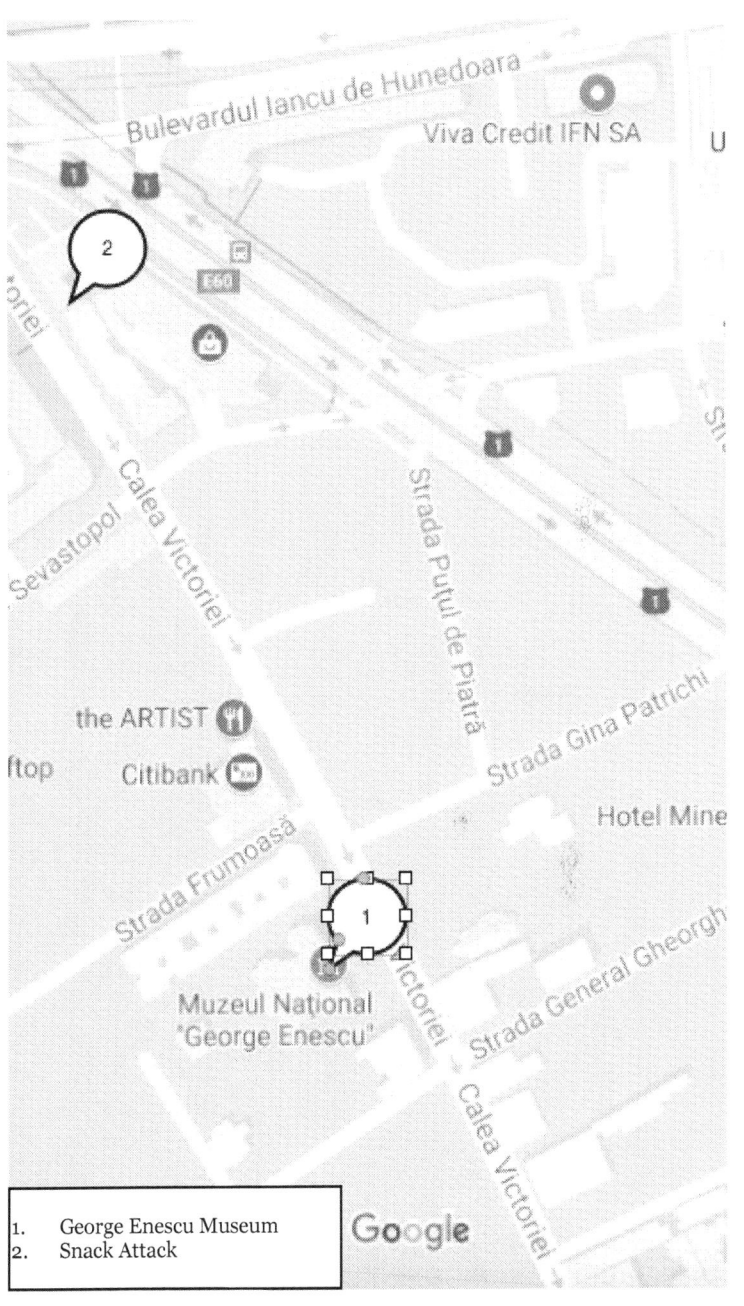

1. George Enescu Museum
2. Snack Attack

THE SINGLE GIRL'S GUIDE TO BUCHAREST

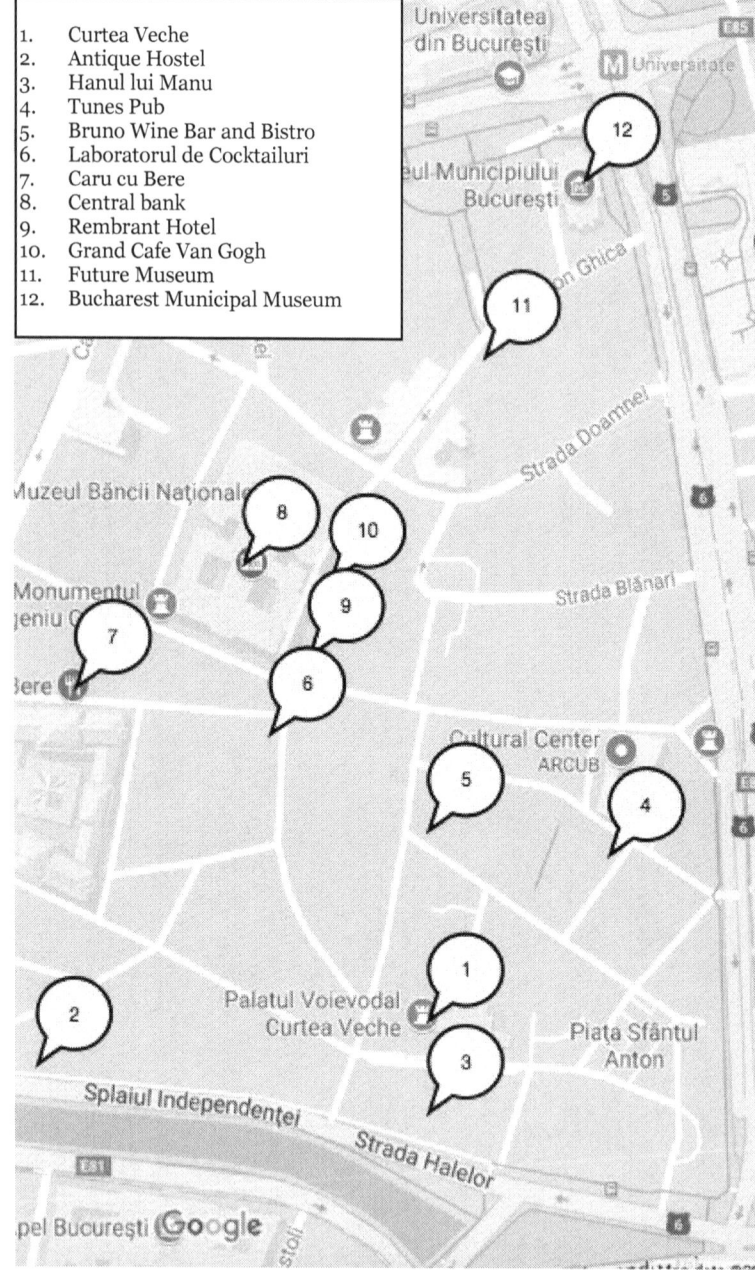

1. Curtea Veche
2. Antique Hostel
3. Hanul lui Manu
4. Tunes Pub
5. Bruno Wine Bar and Bistro
6. Laboratorul de Cocktailuri
7. Caru cu Bere
8. Central bank
9. Rembrant Hotel
10. Grand Cafe Van Gogh
11. Future Museum
12. Bucharest Municipal Museum

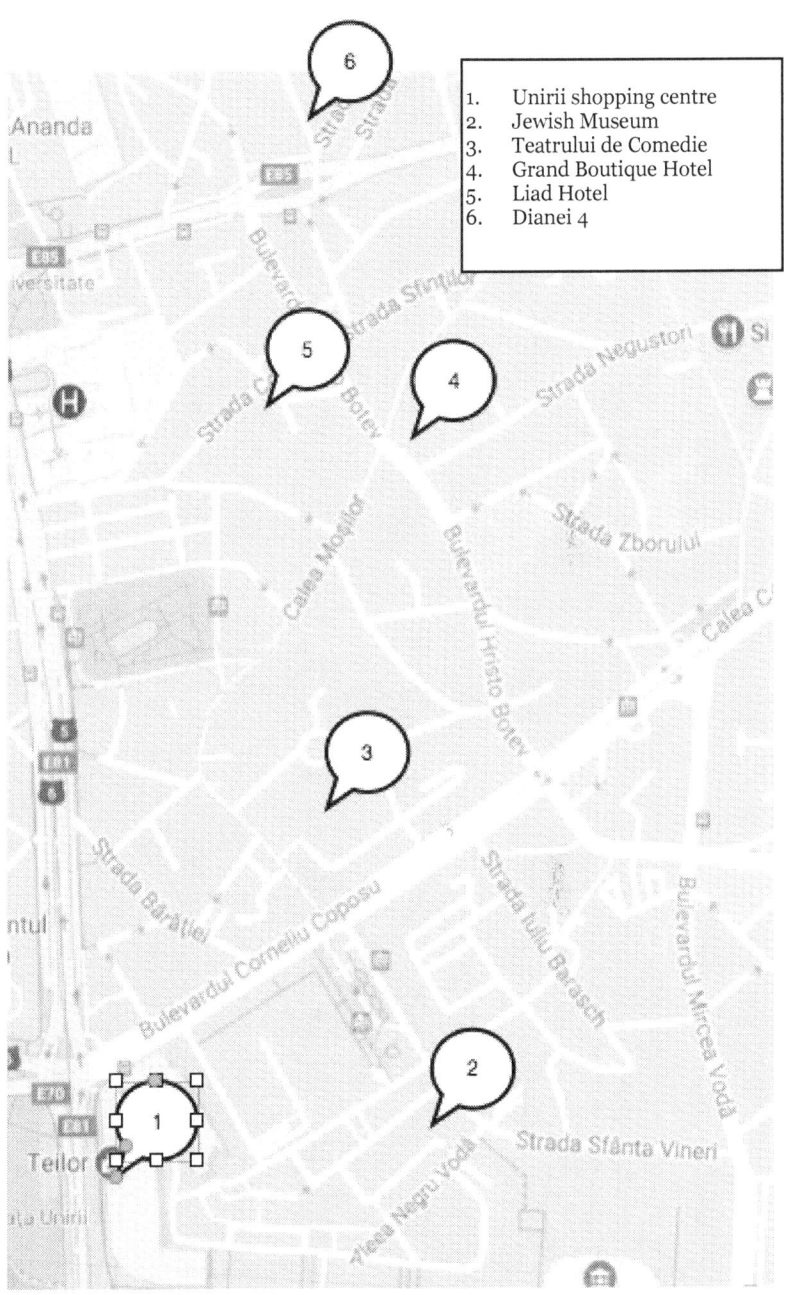

1. Unirii shopping centre
2. Jewish Museum
3. Teatrului de Comedie
4. Grand Boutique Hotel
5. Liad Hotel
6. Dianei 4

THE SINGLE GIRL'S GUIDE TO BUCHAREST

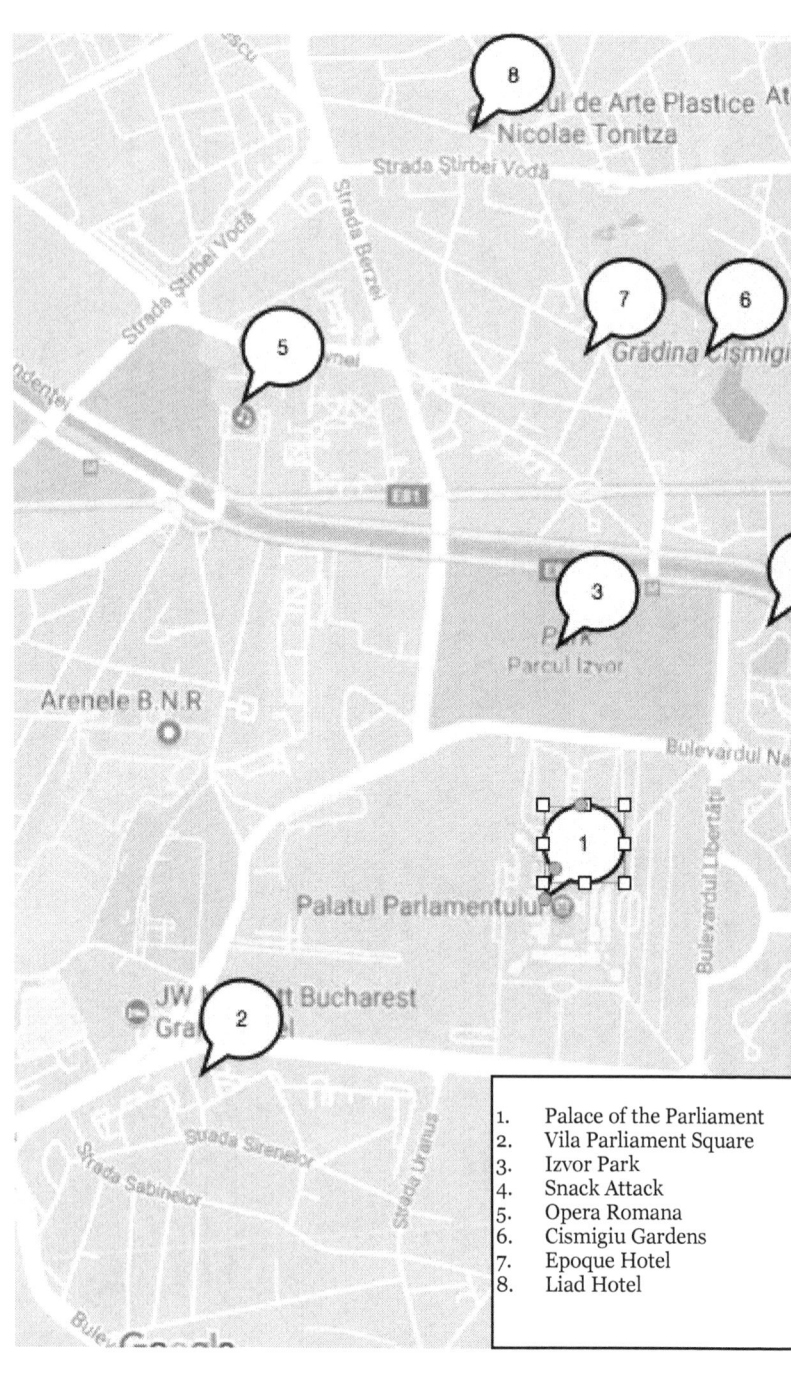

1. Palace of the Parliament
2. Vila Parliament Square
3. Izvor Park
4. Snack Attack
5. Opera Romana
6. Cismigiu Gardens
7. Epoque Hotel
8. Liad Hotel

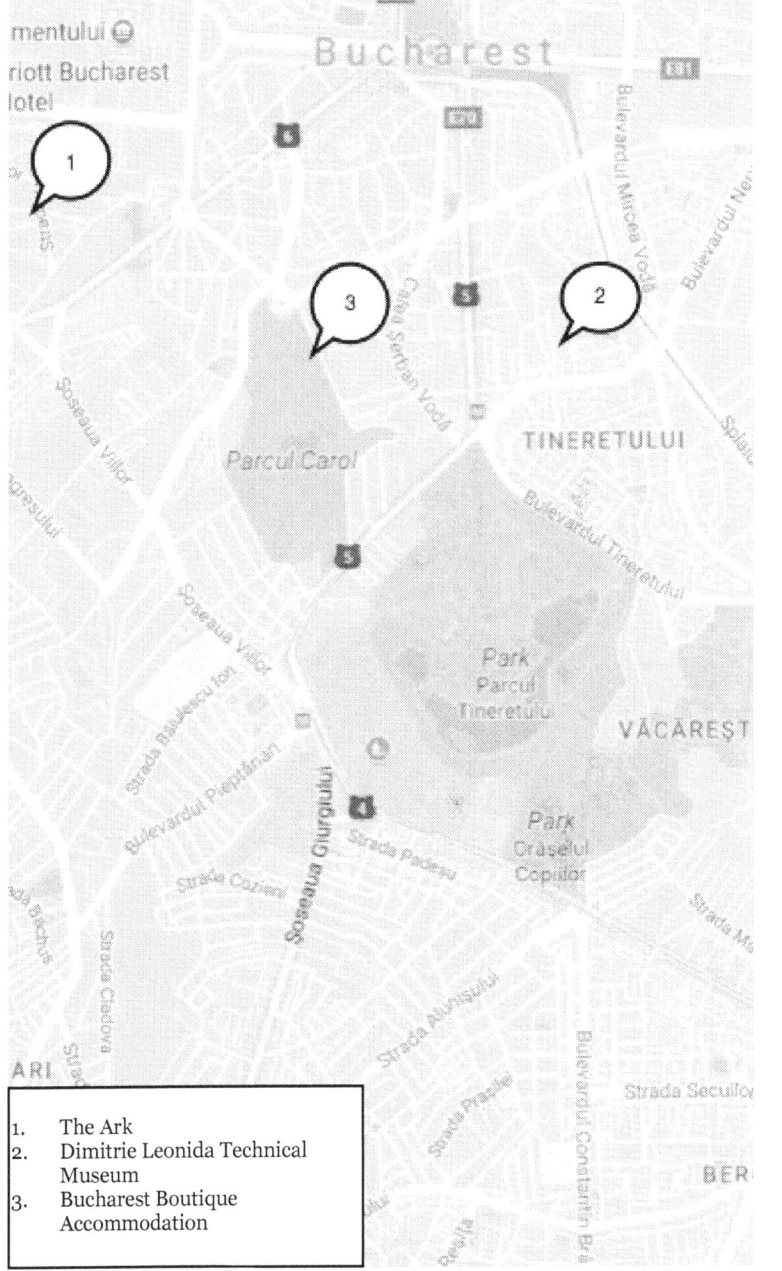

1. The Ark
2. Dimitrie Leonida Technical Museum
3. Bucharest Boutique Accommodation

THE SINGLE GIRL'S GUIDE TO BUCHAREST

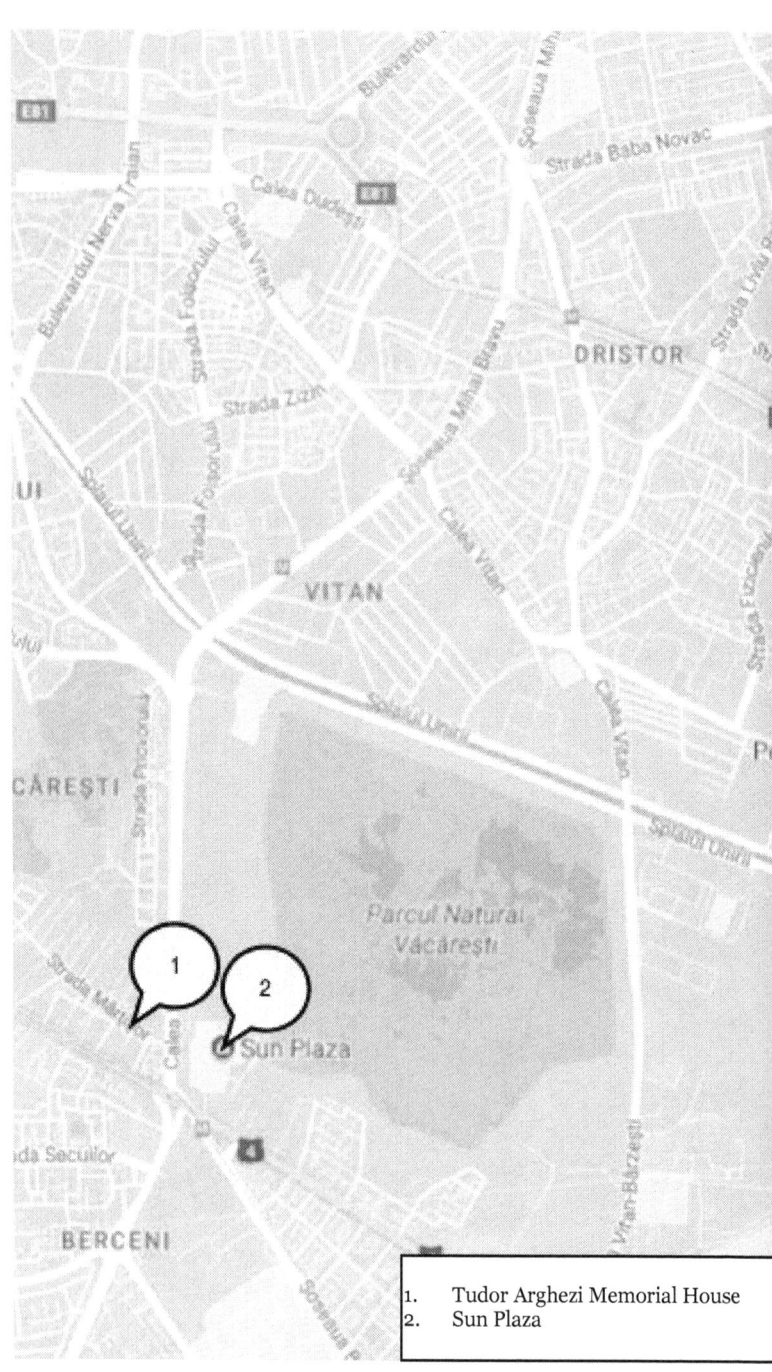

1. Tudor Arghezi Memorial House
2. Sun Plaza

NOTES

18875368R00079

Printed in Poland
by Amazon Fulfillment
Poland Sp. z o.o., Wrocław